The Penguin Book of
CONTEMPORARY
BRITISH POETRY

Edited by
BLAKE MORRISON
and ANDREW MOTION

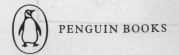

PENGUIN BOOKS

Penguin Books Ltd, Harmondsworth, Middlesex, England
Penguin Books, 40 West 23rd Street, New York, New York 10010, U.S.A.
Penguin Books Australia Ltd, Ringwood, Victoria, Australia
Penguin Books Canada Ltd, 2801 John Street, Markham, Ontario, Canada L3R 1B4
Penguin Books (N.Z.) Ltd, 182–190 Wairau Road, Auckland 10, New Zealand

First published 1982
Reprinted 1982, 1983, 1984

Printed and bound in Great Britain by
Cox & Wyman Ltd, Reading
Set in Linotron 202 Plantin

Contents

8

Contents

Preface

This anthology is intended to be didactic as well as representative. It illustrates what we believe to be the most important achievements and developments in British poetry during recent years. Various practical considerations helped to shape our thoughts. We have not included any work by poets who appeared in the last Penguin anthology of this kind – A. Alvarez's *The New Poetry* (1962). Nor have we included work by poets Alvarez omitted, but who belong to older poetic generations than those we wish to represent. We have decided to give generous selections from relatively few poets rather than small selections from many.

B. M.
A. M.

Introduction

There are points in literary history when decisive shifts of sensibility occur. New, usually aggressive notes are struck; conventions are challenged or broken or simply exposed as being conventions; innovations of form accompany the broaching of unfamiliar subject matter. For a time young poets of very different backgrounds and temperament may feel themselves, or be felt by critics, to be working along similar lines. Though its long-term consequence necessarily remains unclear, such a shift of sensibility has taken place very recently in British poetry. It follows a stretch, occupying much of the 1960s and 70s, when very little – in England at any rate – seemed to be happening, when achievements in British poetry were overshadowed by those in drama and fiction, and when, despite the presence of strong individual writers, there was a lack of overall shape and direction. Now, after a spell of lethargy, British poetry is once again undergoing a transition: a body of work has been created which demands, for its appreciation, a reformation of poetic taste. It is in the belief that this shift is genuine and important, and needs to be brought to the attention of a wider public, that this anthology has been compiled.

We are not, of course, the first anthologists this century to have made such a claim. It is the privilege of every generation to pride itself on having done something remarkable – just as the risk each generation runs is to look ridiculous in the eyes of history. 'English poetry is once again putting on a new strength and beauty': so said Edward Marsh, introducing the first Georgian anthology, in 1912. Similar convictions lay behind Ezra Pound's and Amy Lowell's Imagist anthologies of 1914 and 1915, Michael Roberts's *New Signatures* in 1932, the neo-Apocalyptic anthologies of the early 1940s, Robert Conquest's *New Lines* in 1956, and A. Alvarez's *The New Poetry* in 1962. The word 'new' is conspicuous in all these titles, and making it new is the oldest of all anthologists' arts. In the face of manifesto-making a degree of scepticism is only proper. But it is now twenty years since the last serious anthology of British poetry was published: that – if the cycles of literary history in this century are anything to go by – is an unusually long gap, and to fill it with a representative anthology must in itself be some kind of service. We believe that we may be able to do rather more than that: this is an anthology of what, over the last few years, a number of close observers have come to think of as the new British poetry.

The new spirit in British poetry began to make itself felt in Northern Ireland during the late 1960s and early 70s; more recently, a number of gifted English poets, all under forty, have also emerged. Typically, they show greater imaginative freedom and linguistic daring than the previous poetic generation. Free from the constraints of immediate post-war life, and notwithstanding the threats to their own culture, they have developed a degree of ludic and literary self-consciousness reminiscent of the modernists. This is not to imply that their work is frivolous or amoral. The point is rather that, as a way of making the familiar strange again, they have exchanged the received idea of the poet as the-person-next-door, or knowing insider, for the attitude of the anthropologist or alien invader or remembering exile. (Indeed a number of the poets *are* exiles.) It is a change of outlook which expresses itself, in some poets, in a preference for metaphor and poetic bizzarrerie to metonymy and plain speech; in others it is evident in a renewed interest in narrative – that is, in describing the details and complexities of (often dramatic) incidents, as well as in registering the difficulties and strategies involved in retailing them. It manifests, in other words, a preoccupation with relativism – and this represents a radical departure from the empirical mode which was conspicuous, largely because of Philip Larkin's example, in British poetry of the 1950s and 60s. The new poetry is often open-ended, reluctant to point the moral of, or conclude too neatly, what it chooses to transcribe. And it reasserts the primacy of the imagination in poetry, having come to see the imagination not, as did the previous generation, as part of the dark force of modern history (Hitler, Hiroshima, the Nazi and Soviet camps) but as a potential source of tenderness and renewal.

This development has been antipathetic to the production of a candidly personal poetry. Most of the devices developed by young poets are designed to emphasize the gap between themselves and their subjects. These poets are – to borrow a phrase from Seamus Heaney's 'Exposure' – 'inner emigrés': not inhabitants of their own lives so much as intrigued observers, not victims but onlookers, not poets working in a confessional white heat but dramatists and story-tellers. The point is worth emphasizing because the change has produced a very different kind of poetry from that which Alvarez, in *The New Poetry*, hoped might come about. Our anthology cannot help but be very conscious of Alvarez's: it was enormously influential and its fighting introduction – the attack on 'gentility' and the advocation of the risk-taking poetry of two Americans in the first edition (Robert Lowell, John Berryman), two more in the second, 1965, edition (Sylvia Plath, Anne Sexton), and one Englishman (Ted Hughes) – is rightly famous. But it has become a historical document. The four Americans are dead; Ted Hughes is a remarkable writer but no longer the presiding spirit of British poetry; and Alvarez's insistence that 'the forces of disintegration' be represented in poetry, not hushed up by English decency, has come to seem simplistic. The implication of *The New Poetry* that a correlation necessarily exists between gravity of subject and quality of achievement is one that many young writers – James Fenton for instance – regard with scorn:

> He tells you, in the sombrest notes,
> If poets want to get their oats
> The first step is to slit their throats.
>   The way to divide
> The sheep of poetry from the goats
>   Is suicide.

There is another reason why recent British poetry has taken forms quite other than those promoted by Alvarez: the emergence and example of Seamus Heaney. The most important new poet of the last fifteen years, and the one we very deliberately put first in our anthology, Heaney is someone Alvarez could not foresee at the time and someone he has attacked since. On the face of it, Alvarez's hostility to Heaney's work might seem merely wilful. In fact it is entirely consistent with the attitudes adopted in *The New Poetry*. Alvarez praised Lowell, Hughes, *et al.* for dealing with their experience 'nakedly', and he presented language as a mere instrument in a therapeutic transaction between writer and reader. Heaney is characteristically more oblique; and he delights in language, relishing it – as poems like 'Broagh' make clear – as something that embodies politics, history and locality, as well as having its own delectability.

Heaney's strength and cunning are strikingly evident in what have come to be known as his 'Bog Poems', which refract the experience of the contemporary Irish Troubles through the sufferings of a previous Northern civilization and its sacrificial victims. The Bog people, whose ritually murdered bodies were preserved in peat for centuries, become Heaney's objective correlative. One of the most .famous of this series of poems is 'The Grauballe Man', which describes a subtle and typical process of rehabilitation:

> As if he had been poured
> in tar, he lies
> on a pillow of turf
> and seems to weep
>
> the black river of himself.
> The grain of his wrists
> is like bog oak,
> the ball of his heel
>
> like a basalt egg.
> His instep has shrunk
> cold as a swan's foot
> or a wet swamp root.
>
> His hips are the ridge
> and purse of a mussel,
> his spine an eel arrested
> under a glisten of mud.
>
> The head lifts,
> the chin is a visor
> raised above the vent
> of his slashed throat
>
> that has tanned and toughened.
> The cured wound
> opens inwards to a dark
> elderberry place.
>
> Who will say 'corpse'
> to his vivid cast?
> Who will say 'body'
> to his opaque repose?
>
> And his rusted hair,
> a mat unlikely
> as a foetus's.
> I first saw his twisted face

in a photograph,
a head and shoulder
out of the peat,
bruised like a forceps baby,

but now he lies
perfected in my memory,
down to the red horn
of his nails,

hung in the scales
with beauty and atrocity:
with the Dying Gaul
too strictly compassed

on his shield,
with the actual weight
of each hooded victim
slashed and dumped.

This poem restores the exhumed body to our consciousness in two stages. The first, paradoxically, seems only likely to distance and disperse it. As Heaney's eye ranges over the anatomy it transforms skin and bone to a clutter of inanimate things: the wrist to 'bog oak', the heel to 'a basalt egg', the mortal wound to a 'dark elderberry place', and so on. But this literally objectifying stare is in fact the means towards subjectivity; while asserting the deadness of the corpse by exploring its resemblance to things, Heaney also constructs it again on his own terms. The bog's victim is delivered to a kind of latter life, existing not only as an extraordinary museum piece but as a living commentary on the world it has rejoined. It is a pathetic prophet of contemporary violence, of present-day victims also 'slashed and dumped'. Heaney's process of working in 'The Grauballe Man' has, too, this larger emblematic significance: that it demonstrates how the 'forces of disintegration' which currently confront us are best approached not nakedly and hysterically but with the 'opaque repose' (not to be confused with lack of feeling) that a larger historical framework makes possible. It is a lesson to which a number of his successors have paid attention.

It would be a mistake to think that Heaney has always written in this oblique way. Like a number of other Northern Irish poets, including Derek Mahon and Michael Longley, he served his apprenticeship under Philip Hobsbaum, who taught at Belfast in the early 1960s and whose allegiances were broadly those of the 1950s Movement writers. The Movement virtues of common sense, craftsmanship, and explication are evident in all these poets' early work, and it is only gradually that they have evolved a more symbolic and associative mode. Heaney's confederacy with Mahon, Longley and others – the presence, that is, of a Belfast 'group' – is one of the reasons why he must not be seen in isolation. Though he is the pre-eminent figure, he has not carried out the so-called Northern Irish 'Renaissance' single-handed. To understand what has been achieved in Ulster one should also look at poems like Mahon's 'A Disused Shed in Co. Wexford', Longley's 'Wounds', Paul Muldoon's 'Immram', Tom Paulin's 'The Harbour in the Evening' and Medbh McGuckian's 'The Flitting'. It is interesting to speculate on the relationship between the resurgence of Northern Irish writing and the Troubles. The poets have all experienced a sense of 'living in important places' and have been under considerable pressure to 'respond'. They have been brought hard up against questions about the relationship between art and politics, between the private and the public, between conscious 'making' and intuitive 'inspiration'. But on the whole they have avoided a poetry of directly documentary reportage. Love poems and domestic poems – Longley's 'The Linen Workers', for example – have been made to accommodate an uncommonly wide range of social responsiveness, while some poets have looked to other cultures as a way of putting the immediate and circumstantial into a wider perspective. Heaney's Bog Poems are an obvious example, and a similar purpose is fulfilled by Mahon's archaeological digs, Muldoon's Chandleresque travels and Paulin's recreations of early twentieth-century Russia.

So impressive is recent Northern Irish poetry (six poets from the North are included here and several others might also have been) that it is not surprising to find discussions of English poetry so often having to take place in its shadow. This is not the first time this has happened. In 'How To Read' (1928) Ezra Pound claimed that 'the language is now in the keeping of the Irish'. But just as Auden and others rescued the reputation of English poetry in the 1930s, so in the 1970s and 80s a new generation of poets has started to do the same. Two key figures are Douglas Dunn and Tony Harrison, who are sharply conscious of a background

and upbringing which sets them at an angle to the cultural estab-
lishment. Dunn's 'Barbarians' and Harrison's 'Rhubarbarians'
bear grudges against what Dunn calls 'a culture of connivance,/
Of "authority", arts of bland recoveries', and both writers insist
on the strength and value of their alternative traditions, which are
provincial and working-class. But rather than reject establishment
culture altogether, Dunn and Harrison adapt and vary its poetic
forms for their own ends. This tension neatly expresses one of
their dominant themes: the sense that in learning to be poetically
articulate they have become cut off from their backgrounds. The
poignancy of the working-class writer's separation from his
community is humorously handled in Harrison's 'Me Tarzan':

> Outside the whistled gang-call, *Twelfth Street Rag*,
> then a Tarzan yodel for the kid who's bored,
> whose hand's on his liana . . . no, back
> to Labienus and his flaming sword.
>
> *Off laikin', then to t'fish'oil* all the boys,
> *off tartin', off to t'flicks* but on, on, on,
> the foldaway card-table, the green baize,
> *De Bello Gallico* and lexicon.
>
> It's only his jaw muscles that he's tensed
> into an enraged *shit* that he can't go;
> down with polysyllables, he's against
> all pale-faced Caesars, *for* Geronimo.
>
> He shoves the frosted attic skylight, shouts:
>
> *Ah bloody can't ah've gorra Latin prose.*
>
> His bodiless head that's poking out's
> like patriarchal Sissy-bleeding-ro's.

Along with Jeffrey Wainwright, Dunn and Harrison show an
awareness of economic and class differences which suggests that
the Irish poets are far from being the only ones lately to have con-
cerned themselves with political matters. But while their social
commitment is indisputable, they recognize that it need not take
the form of earnest moralizing. The linguistic games of Harrison's
recent poetry are often extremely elaborate, while Dunn has been
increasingly drawn to the kind of expansive fictionalizing evident
in 'An Artist Waiting in a Country House'. It is this recognition
which associates Dunn and Harrison with another development of

English poetry of the last few years, one which in other respects might seem strikingly dissimilar: the 'Martian' school.

The name was taken from Craig Raine's 'A Martian Sends a Postcard Home', a poem in which the familiar world is seen through the eyes of a fascinated alien:

> Only the young are allowed to suffer
> openly. Adults go to a punishment room
>
> with water but nothing to eat.
> They lock the door and suffer the noises
>
> alone. No one is exempt...

Where Heaney, Harrison and Dunn have extended the boundaries of their work gradually over a number of years, Raine asserted his freedom immediately and with spectacular confidence. The same is true of Christopher Reid, whose first book, like Raine's, was published in the late 1970s and instantly identified as 'Martian'. Although two substantially different poetic personalities, Raine and Reid share a delight in outrageous simile and like to twist and mix language in order to revive the ordinary. Both refer a good deal to children, for this is one way of viewing the commonplace with wonder and innocence. In many respects their work seems to fit Dr Johnson's description of Metaphysical poetry – 'heterogeneous ideas... yoked by violence together'. To put it another way: they have demonstrated that if a poem draws a line round an incident or area of experience, observations which fall within its circumference seek each other out and establish relationships. Though such connections and relationships are artfully arranged, it would be wrong to think that the Martians' ingenuity prevents them from expressing emotion: their way of looking is also a way of feeling. It is a point which other poets have begun to recognize and explains why Raine and Reid have proved so influential in a comparatively short time. What might, a few years ago, have looked far-fetched and fanciful now appears as part of a new confidence in the poetic imagination. The work of David Sweetman, Medbh McGuckian and Penelope Shuttle provides further examples of this opening out in British poetry.

Whereas Raine and Reid re-interpret the world through their use of simile, a number of other young poets have done so through the art of narrative. This, again, is not so much a new element in poetry as an isolation and re-emphasis of a time-honoured

one. An interest in narrative has always been a feature of poetry
and particularly of 'poetic revolutions'. But one important differ-
ence between its adoption today and its use by – say – Words-
worth or Tennyson or Frost is that contemporary poets write
their stories with more reference to what the process involves.
The fact of fictionalizing is relished as it is performed. James
Fenton gives a good example of this in his 'A Vacant Possession':

> The difficult guest is questioning his rival.
> He is pacing up and down while she leans against
> A mossy water-butt in which, could we see them,
> Innumerable forms of life are uncurving.

By registering the degree to which the poem is an invention, and
creates its own world – neither guest, nor companion, nor writer
nor reader can see the 'innumerable forms of life' which are said
to be there – Fenton draws attention to the artifice and autonomy
of his text. Where other poets make the familiar strange again
through linguistic and metaphoric play, the young narrative poets
perform a similar function by drawing attention to the problem of
perception. In poems by Fenton and Paulin and Muldoon and
others, we are often presented with stories that are incomplete, or
are denied what might normally be considered essential informa-
tion. The reader is constantly being made to ask, 'Who is speak-
ing?', 'What are their circumstances and motives?' and 'Can they
be believed?' There is, moreover, leisure to ponder these ques-
tions at length. After a period of dominance by the short lyric,
the art of the long poem – whether unbroken like Muldoon's
'Immram' or in a sequence like Anne Stevenson's *Correspondences*
and Jeffrey Wainwright's 'Thomas Müntzer' – is once again being
explored. The pressures of space in magazine outlets for poetry
endanger the survival of the long poem, but a number of young
poets today take the view once expressed by Keats:

> Do not the Lovers of Poetry like to have a little Region to
> wander in where they may pick and choose, and where
> images are so numerous that many are forgotten and found
> new in a second Reading: which may be food for a Week's
> stroll in the Summer? Do not they like this better than
> what they can read through before Mrs Williams comes
> down stairs? a Morning work at most. Besides a long Poem is
> a test of Invention which I take to be the Polar Star of

Poetry, as Fancy is the Sails, and Imagination the Rudder. Did our great Poets ever write short pieces? I mean in the shape of Tales – This same invention seems indeed of late Years to have been forgotten as a Poetical excellence.

In pressing the claims of the poets who have emerged in the last fifteen years or so, we do not wish to under-estimate the achievement or influence of their predecessors. Heaney's literary relationship with Lowell and Ted Hughes, for instance, or Dunn's with Larkin – such debts are crucial, and it would clearly be wrong to pretend there had been any absolute break with the past. But the poets included here do represent a departure, one which may be said to exhibit something of the spirit of post-modernism. And though there are, as we have emphasized, a number of different 'schools' and tendencies at work in the anthology, and while all the poets have distinct and distinguished individual talents, what we are struck by powerfully is the sense of common purpose: to extend the imaginative franchise.

SEAMUS HEANEY

Churning Day

A thick crust, coarse-grained as limestone rough-cast,
hardened gradually on top of the four crocks
that stood, large pottery bombs, in the small pantry.
After the hot brewery of gland, cud and udder
cool porous earthenware fermented the buttermilk
for churning day, when the hooped churn was scoured
with plumping kettles and the busy scrubber
echoed daintily on the seasoned wood.
It stood then, purified, on the flagged kitchen floor.

Out came the four crocks, spilled their heavy lip
of cream, their white insides, into the sterile churn.
The staff, like a great whisky muddler fashioned
in deal wood, was plunged in, the lid fitted.
My mother took first turn, set up rhythms
that slugged and thumped for hours. Arms ached.
Hands blistered. Cheeks and clothes were spattered
with flabby milk.

            Where finally gold flecks
began to dance. They poured hot water then,
sterilized a birchwood-bowl
and little corrugated butter-spades.
Their short stroke quickened, suddenly
a yellow curd was weighting the churned up white,
heavy and rich, coagulated sunlight
that they fished, dripping, in a wide tin strainer,
heaped up like gilded gravel in the bowl.

The house would stink long after churning day,
acrid as a sulphur mine. The empty crocks
were ranged along the wall again, the butter
in soft printed slabs was piled on pantry shelves.
And in the house we moved with gravid ease,
our brains turned crystals full of clean deal churns,
the plash and gurgle of the sour-breathed milk,
the pat and slap of small spades on wet lumps.

At Ardboe Point

Right along the lough shore
A smoke of flies
Drifts thick in the sunset.

They come smattering daintily
Against the windscreen,
The grill and bonnet whisper

At their million collisions:
It is to drive through
A hail of fine chaff.

Yet we leave no clear wake
For they open and close on us
As the air opens and closes.

To-night when we put out our light
To kiss between sheets
Their just audible siren will go

Outside the window,
Their invisible veil
Weakening the moonlight still further

And the walls will carry a rash
Of them, a green pollen.
They'll have infiltrated our clothes by morning.

If you put one under a lens
You'd be looking at a pumping body
With such outsize beaters for wings

That this visitation would seem
More drastic than Pharaoh's –
I'm told they're mosquitoes

But I'd need forests and swamps
To believe it
For these are our innocent, shuttling

Choirs, dying through
Their own live empyrean, troublesome only
As the last veil on a dancer.

Broagh

Riverbank, the long rigs
ending in broad docken
and a canopied pad
down to the ford.

The garden mould
bruised easily, the shower
gathering in your heelmark
was the black *O*

in *Broagh*,
its low tattoo
among the windy boortrees
and rhubarb-blades

ended almost
suddenly, like that last
gh the strangers found
difficult to manage.

Anahorish

My 'place of clear water',
the first hill in the world
where springs washed into
the shiny grass

and darkened cobbles
in the bed of the lane.
Anahorish, soft gradient
of consonant, vowel-meadow,

after-image of lamps
swung through the yards
on winter evenings.
With pails and barrows

those mound-dwellers
go waist-deep in mist
to break the light ice
at wells and dunghills.

Mossbawn: Two Poems in Dedication
for Mary Heaney

1. Sunlight

There was a sunlit absence.
The helmeted pump in the yard
heated its iron,
water honeyed

in the slung bucket
and the sun stood
like a griddle cooling
against the wall

of each long afternoon.
So, her hands scuffled
over the bakeboard,
the reddening stove

sent its plaque of heat
against her where she stood
in a floury apron
by the window.

Now she dusts the board
with a goose's wing,
now sits, broad-lapped,
with whitened nails

and measling shins:
here is a space
again, the scone rising
to the tick of two clocks.

And here is love
like a tinsmith's scoop
sunk past its gleam
in the meal-bin.

2. The Seed Cutters

They seem hundreds of years away. Breughel,
You'll know them if I get them true.
They kneel under the hedge in a half-circle
Behind a windbreak wind is breaking through.

They are the seed cutters. The tuck and frill
Of leaf-sprout is on the seed potatoes
Buried under that straw. With time to kill
They are taking their time. Each sharp knife goes
Lazily halving each root that falls apart
In the palm of the hand: a milky gleam,
And, at the centre, a dark watermark.
O calendar customs! Under the broom
Yellowing over them, compose the frieze
With all of us there, our anonymities.

Funeral Rites

I

I shouldered a kind of manhood
stepping in to lift the coffins
of dead relations.
They had been laid out

in tainted rooms,
their eyelids glistening,
their dough-white hands
shackled in rosary beads.

Their puffed knuckles
had unwrinkled, the nails
were darkened, the wrists
obediently sloped.

The dulse-brown shroud,
the quilted satin cribs:
I knelt courteously
admiring it all

as wax melted down
and veined the candles,
the flames hovering
to the women hovering

behind me.
And always, in a corner,
the coffin lid,
its nail-heads dressed

with little gleaming crosses.
Dear soapstone masks,
kissing their igloo brows
had to suffice

before the nails were sunk
and the black glacier
of each funeral
pushed away.

II

Now as news comes in
of each neighbourly murder
we pine for ceremony,
customary rhythms:

the temperate footsteps
of a cortège, winding past
each blinded home.
I would restore

the great chambers of Boyne,
prepare a sepulchre
under the cupmarked stones.
Out of side-streets and bye-roads

purring family cars
nose into line,
the whole country tunes
to the muffled drumming

of ten thousand engines.
Somnambulant women,
left behind, move
through emptied kitchens

imagining our slow triumph
towards the mounds.
Quiet as a serpent
in its grassy boulevard

the procession drags its tail
out of the Gap of the North
as its head already enters
the megalithic doorway.

III

When they have put the stone
back in its mouth
we will drive north again
past Strang and Carling fjords

the cud of memory
allayed for once, arbitration
of the feud placated,
imagining those under the hill

disposed like Gunnar
who lay beautiful
inside his burial mound,
though dead by violence

and unavenged.
Men said that he was chanting
verses about honour
and that four lights burned

in corners of the chamber:
which opened then, as he turned
with a joyful face
to look at the moon.

The Tollund Man

I

Some day I will go to Aarhus
To see his peat-brown head,
The mild pods of his eye-lids,
His pointed skin cap.

In the flat country nearby
Where they dug him out,
His last gruel of winter seeds
Caked in his stomach,

Naked except for
The cap, noose and girdle,

I will stand a long time.
Bridegroom to the goddess,

She tightened her torc on him
And opened her fen,
Those dark juices working
Him to a saint's kept body,

Trove of the turfcutters'
Honeycombed workings
Now his stained face
Reposes at Aarhus.

II

I could risk blasphemy,
Consecrate the cauldron bog
Our holy ground and pray
Him to make germinate

The scattered, ambushed
Flesh of labourers,
Stockinged corpses
Laid out in the farmyards

Tell-tale skin and teeth
Flecking the sleepers
Of four young brothers, trailed
For miles along the lines.

III

Something of his sad freedom
As he rode the tumbril
Should come to me, driving,
Saying the names

Tollund, Grauballe, Nebelgard,
Watching the pointing hands
Of country people,
Not knowing their tongue.

Out there in Jutland
In the old man-killing parishes
I will feel lost,
Unhappy and at home.

Punishment

I can feel the tug
of the halter at the nape
of her neck, the wind
on her naked front.

It blows her nipples
to amber beads,
it shakes the frail rigging
of her ribs.

I can see her drowned
body in the bog,
the weighing stone,
the floating rods and boughs.

Under which at first
she was a barked sapling
that is dug up
oak-bone, brain-firkin:

her shaved head
like a stubble of black corn,
her blindfold a soiled bandage,
her noose a ring

to store
the memories of love.
Little adulteress,
before they punished you

you were flaxen-haired,
undernourished, and your
tar-black face was beautiful.
My poor scapegoat,

I almost love you
but would have cast, I know,
the stones of silence.
I am the artful voyeur

of your brain's exposed
and darkened combs,

your muscles' webbing
and all your numbered bones:

I who have stood dumb
when your betraying sisters,
cauled in tar,
wept by the railings,

who would connive
in civilized outrage
yet understand the exact
and tribal, intimate revenge.

Strange Fruit

Here is the girl's head like an exhumed gourd.
Oval-faced, prune-skinned, prune-stones for teeth.
They unswaddled the wet fern of her hair
And made an exhibition of its coil,
Let the air at her leathery beauty.
Pash of tallow, perishable treasure:
Her broken nose is dark as a turf clod,
Her eyeholes blank as pools in the old workings.
Diodorus Siculus confessed
His gradual ease among the likes of this:
Murdered, forgotten, nameless, terrible
Beheaded girl, outstaring axe
And beatification, outstaring
What had begun to feel like reverence.

from Singing School

A Constable Calls

His bicycle stood at the window-sill,
The rubber cowl of a mud-splasher
Skirting the front mudguard,
Its fat black handlegrips

Heating in sunlight, the 'spud'

Of the dynamo gleaming and cocked back,
The pedal treads hanging relieved
Of the boot of the law.

His cap was upside down
On the floor, next his chair.
The line of its pressure ran like a bevel
In his slightly sweating hair.

He had unstrapped
The heavy ledger, and my father
Was making tillage returns
In acres, roods, and perches.

Arithmetic and fear.
I sat staring at the polished holster
With its buttoned flap, the braid cord
Looped into the revolver butt.

'Any other root crops?
Mangolds? Marrowstems? Anything like that?'
'No.' But was there not a line
Of turnips where the seed ran out

In the potato field? I assumed
Small guilts and sat
Imagining the black hole in the barracks.
He stood up, shifted the baton-case

Further round on his belt,
Closed the domesday book,
Fitted his cap back with two hands,
And looked at me as he said goodbye.

A shadow bobbed in the window.
He was snapping the carrier spring
Over the ledger. His boot pushed off
And the bicycle ticked, ticked, ticked.

Exposure

It is December in Wicklow:
Alders dripping, birches
Inheriting the last light,
The ash tree cold to look at.

A comet that was lost
Should be visible at sunset,
Those million tons of light
Like a glimmer of haws and rose-hips,

And I sometimes see a falling star.
If I could come on meteorite!
Instead I walk through damp leaves,
Husks, the spent flukes of autumn,

Imagining a hero
On some muddy compound,
His gift like a slingstone
Whirled for the desperate.

How did I end up like this?
I often think of my friends'
Beautiful prismatic counselling
And the anvil brains of some who hate me

As I sit weighing and weighing
My responsible *tristia*.
For what? For the ear? For the people?
For what is said behind-backs?

Rain comes down through the alders,
Its low conducive voices
Mutter about let-downs and erosions
And yet each drop recalls

The diamond absolutes.
I am neither internee nor informer;
An inner émigré, grown long-haired
And thoughtful; a wood-kerne

Escaped from the massacre,
Taking protective colouring
From bole and bark, feeling
Every wind that blows;

Who, blowing up these sparks
For their meagre heat, have missed
The once-in-a-lifetime portent,
The comet's pulsing rose.

Casualty

I

He would drink by himself
And raise a weathered thumb
Towards the high shelf,
Calling another rum
And blackcurrant, without
Having to raise his voice,
Or order a quick stout
By a lifting of the eyes
And a discreet dumb-show
Of pulling off the top;
At closing time would go
In waders and peaked cap
Into the showery dark,
A dole-kept breadwinner
But a natural for work.
I loved his whole manner,
Sure-footed but too sly,
His deadpan sidling tact,
His fisherman's quick eye
And turned observant back.

Incomprehensible
To him, my other life.
Sometimes, on his high stool,
Too busy with his knife
At a tobacco plug
And not meeting my eye,
In the pause after a slug
He mentioned poetry.
We would be on our own
And, always politic
And shy of condescension,
I would manage by some trick
To switch the talk to eels
Or lore of the horse and cart
Or the Provisionals.

But my tentative art

His turned back watches too:
He was blown to bits
Out drinking in a curfew
Others obeyed, three nights
After they shot dead
The thirteen men in Derry.
PARAS THIRTEEN, the walls said,
BOGSIDE NIL. That Wednesday
Everybody held
His breath and trembled.

II

It was a day of cold
Raw silence, wind-blown
Surplice and soutane:
Rained-on, flower-laden
Coffin after coffin
Seemed to float from the door
Of the packed cathedral
Like blossoms on slow water.
The common funeral
Unrolled its swaddling band,
Lapping, tightening
Till we were braced and bound
Like brothers in a ring.

But he would not be held
At home by his own crowd
Whatever threats were phoned,
Whatever black flags waved.
I see him as he turned
In that bombed offending place,
Remorse fused with terror
In his still knowable face,
His cornered outfaced stare
Blinding in the flash.

He had gone miles away
For he drank like a fish
Nightly, naturally
Swimming towards the lure
Of warm lit-up places,

The blurred mesh and murmur
Drifting among glasses
In the gregarious smoke.
How culpable was he
That last night when he broke
Our tribe's complicity?
'Now you're supposed to be
An educated man,'
I hear him say. 'Puzzle me
The right answer to that one.'

III

I missed his funeral,
Those quiet walkers
And sideways talkers
Shoaling out of his lane
To the respectable
Purring of the hearse . . .
They move in equal pace
With the habitual
Slow consolation
Of a dawdling engine,
The line lifted, hand
Over fist, cold sunshine
On the water, the land
Banked under fog: that morning
I was taken in his boat,
The screw purling, turning
Indolent fathoms white,
I tasted freedom with him.
To get out early, haul
Steadily off the bottom,
Dispraise the catch, and smile
As you find a rhythm
Working you, slow mile by mile,
Into your proper haunt
Somewhere, well out, beyond . . .

Dawn-sniffing revenant,
Plodder through midnight rain,
Question me again.

The Harvest Bow

As you plaited the harvest bow
You implicated the mellowed silence in you
In wheat that does not rust
But brightens as it tightens twist by twist
Into a knowable corona,
A throwaway love-knot of straw.

Hands that aged round ashplants and cane sticks
And lapped the spurs on a lifetime of game cocks
Harked to their gift and worked with fine intent
Until your fingers moved somnambulant:
I tell and finger it like braille,
Gleaning the unsaid off the palpable,

And if I spy into its golden loops
I see us walk between the railway slopes
Into an evening of long grass and midges,
Blue smoke straight up, old beds and ploughs in hedges,
An auction notice on an outhouse wall –
You with a harvest bow in your lapel,

Me with the fishing rod, already homesick
For the big lift of these evenings, as your stick
Whacking the tips off weeds and bushes
Beats out of time, and beats, but flushes
Nothing: that original townland
Still tongue-tied in the straw tied by your hand.

The end of art is peace
Could be the motto of this frail device
That I have pinned up on our deal dresser –
Like a drawn snare
Slipped lately by the spirit of the corn
Yet burnished by its pasage, and still warm.

The Otter

When you plunged
The light of Tuscany wavered
And swung through the pool
From top to bottom.

I loved your wet head and smashing crawl,
Your fine swimmer's back and shoulders
Surfacing and surfacing again
This year and every year since.

I sat dry-throated on the warm stones.
You were beyond me.
The mellowed clarities, the grape-deep air
Thinned and disappointed.

Thank God for the slow loadening,
When I hold you now
We are close and deep
As the atmosphere on water.

My two hands are plumbed water.
You are my palpable, lithe
Otter of memory
In the pool of the moment,

Turning to swim on your back,
Each silent, thigh-shaking kick
Re-tilting the light,
Heaving the cool at your neck.

And suddenly you're out,
Back again, intent as ever,
Heavy and frisky in your freshened pelt,
Printing the stones.

from Glanmore Sonnets
for Ann Saddlemeyer
our heartiest welcomer

I

Vowels ploughed into other: opened ground.
The mildest February for twenty years
Is mist bands over furrows, a deep no sound
Vulnerable to distant gargling tractors.
Our road is steaming, the turned-up acres breathe.
Now the good life could be to cross a field
And art a paradigm of earth new from the lathe
Of ploughs. My lea is deeply tilled.
Old ploughsocks gorge the subsoil of each sense
And I am quickened with a redolence
Of the fundamental dark unblown rose.
Wait then . . . Breasting the mist, in sowers' aprons,
My ghosts come striding into their spring stations.
The dream grain whirls like freakish Easter snows.

V

Soft corrugations in the boortree's trunk,
Its green young shoots, its rods like freckled solder:
It was our bower as children, a greenish, dank
And snapping memory as I get older.
And elderberry I have learned to call it.
I love its blooms like saucers brimmed with meal,
Its berries a swart caviar of shot,
A buoyant spawn, a light bruised out of purple.
Elderberry? It is shires dreaming wine.
Boortree is bower tree, where I played 'touching tongues'
And felt another's texture quick on mine.
So, etymologist of roots and graftings,
I fall back to my tree-house and would crouch
Where small buds shoot and flourish in the hush.

VIII

Thunderlight on the split logs: big raindrops
At body heat and lush with omen
Spattering dark on the hatchet iron.
This morning when a magpie with jerky steps
Inspected a horse asleep beside the wood
I thought of dew on armour and carrion.
What would I meet, blood-boltered, on the road?
How deep into the woodpile sat the toad?
What welters through this dark hush on the crops?
Do you remember that pension in *Les Landes*
Where the old one rocked and rocked and rocked
A mongol in her lap, to little songs?
Come to me quick, I am upstairs shaking.
My all of you birchwood in lightning.

X

I dreamt we slept in a moss in Donegal
On turf banks under blankets, with our faces
Exposed all night in a wetting drizzle,
Pallid as the dripping sapling birches.
Lorenzo and Jessica in a cold climate.
Diarmuid and Grainne waiting to be found.
Darkly asperged and censed, we were laid out
Like breathing effigies on a raised ground.
And in that dream I dreamt – how like you this? –
Our first night years ago in that hotel
When you came with your deliberate kiss
To raise us towards the lovely and painful
Covenants of flesh; our separateness;
The respite in our dewy dreaming faces.

Leavings

A soft whoosh, the sunset blaze
of straw on blackened stubble,
a thatch-deep, freshening
barbarous crimson burn –

I rode down England
as they fired the crop
that was the leavings of a crop,
the smashed tow-coloured barley,

down from Ely's Lady Chapel,
the sweet tenor latin
forever banished,
the sumptuous windows

threshed clear by Thomas Cromwell.
Which circle does he tread,
scalding on cobbles,
each one a broken statue's head?

After midnight, after summer,
to walk in a sparking field,
to smell dew and ashes
and start Will Brangwen's ghost

from the hot soot –
a breaking sheaf of light,
abroad in the hiss
and clash of stooking.

TONY HARRISON

The Nuptial Torches

> *These human victims, chained and burning*
> *at the stake, were the blazing torches*
> *which lighted the monarch to his nuptial couch.*
> (J. L. MOTLEY, *The Rise of the Dutch Republic*)

Fish gnaw the Flushing capons, hauled from fleeced
Lutheran Holland, for tomorrow's feast.
The Netherlandish lengths, the Dutch heirlooms,
That might have graced my movements and my groom's
Fade on the fat sea's bellies where they hung
Like cover-sluts. Flesh, wet linen wrung
Bone dry in a washerwoman's raw, red,
Twisting hands, bed-clothes off a lovers' bed,
Falls off the chains. At Valladolid
It fell, flesh crumpled like a coverlid.

Young Carlos de Sessa stripped was good
For a girl to look at and he spat like wood
Green from the orchards for the cooking pots.
Flames ravelled up his flesh into dry knots
And he cried at the King: *How can you stare*
On such agonies and not turn a hair?
The King was cool: *My friend, I'd drag the logs*
Out to the stake for my own son, let dogs
Get at his testes for his sins; auto-da-fés
Owe no paternity to evil ways.
Cabrera leans against the throne, guffaws
And jots down to the Court's applause
Yet another of the King's *bon mots*.

O yellow piddle in fresh fallen snow –
Dogs on the Guadarramas . . . dogs. Their souls
Splut through their pores like porridge holes.
They wear their skins like cast-offs. Their skin grows
Puckered round the knees like rumpled hose.

Doctor Ponce de la Fuente, you,
Whose gaudy, straw-stuffed effigy in lieu

Of members hacked up in the prison, burns
Here now, one sacking arm drops off, one turns
A stubble finger and your skull still croons
Lascivious catches and indecent tunes;
And croaks: *Ashes to ashes, dust to dust.*
Pray God be with you in your lust.
And God immediately is, but such a one
Whose skin stinks like a herring in the sun,
Huge from confinement in a filthy gaol,
Crushing the hooping on my farthingale.

O Holy Mother, Holy Mother, Ho-
ly Mother Church, whose melodious, low
Labour-moans go through me as you bear
These pitch-stained children to the upper air,
Let them lie still tonight, no crowding smoke
Condensing back to men float in and poke
Their charcoaled fingers at our bed, and let
Me be his pleasure, though Philip sweat
At his rhythms and use those hateful tricks
They say he feels like after heretics.

O let the King be gentle and not loom
Like Torquemada in the torture room,
Those wiry Spanish hairs, these nuptial nights,
Crackling like lit tapers in his tights,
His seed like water spluttered off hot stone.
Maria, whose dark eyes very like my own
Shine on such consummations, Maria bless
My Philip just this once with gentleness.

The King's cool knuckles on my smoky hair!

Mare Mediterraneum, la mer, la mer
That almost got him in your gorge with sides
Of feastmeats, you must flush this scared bride's
Uterus with scouring salt. O cure and cool
The scorching birthmarks of his branding-tool.

Sweat chills my small breasts and limp hands.

They curled like foetuses, *maman*, and cried.

His crusted tunics crumple as he stands:

Come, Isabella. God *is satisfied.*

On Not Being Milton
for Sergio Vieira & Armando Guebuza (Frelimo)

Read and committed to the flames, I call
these sixteen lines that go back to my roots
my *Cahier d'un retour au pays natal*
my growing black enough to fit my boots.

The stutter of the scold out of the branks
of condescension, class and counter-class
thickens with glottals to a lumpen mass
of Ludding morphemes closing up their ranks.
Each swung cast-iron Enoch[1] of Leeds stress
clangs a forged music on the frames of Art,
the looms of owned language smashed apart!

Three cheers for mute ingloriousness!

Articulation is the tongue-tied's fighting.
In the silence round all poetry we quote
Tidd the Cato Street conspirator who wrote:

Sir, I Ham a very Bad Hand at Righting.

1. An 'Enoch' is an iron sledge-hammer used by the Luddites to smash
the frames which were also made by the same Enoch Taylor of Marsden.
The cry was: Enoch made them, Enoch shall break them!

The Rhubarbarians

I

Those glottals glugged like poured pop, each
rebarbative syllable, remembrancer, raise
'mob' *rhubarb-rhubarb* to a tribune's speech
crossing the crackle as the hayricks blaze.

The gaffers' blackleg Boswells at their side.
Horsfall of Ottiwells, if the bugger could,
'd've liked to (exact words recorded) *ride
up to my saddle-girths in Luddite blood.*

What t'mob said to the cannons on the mills,
shouted to soldier, scab and sentinel

's silence, parries and hush on whistling hills,
shadows in moonlight playing knurr and spell.

It wasn't poetry though. Nay, wiseowl Leeds
pro rege et lege schools, nobody needs
your drills and chanting to parrot right
the *tusky-tusky*[1] of the pikes that night.

II
(On translating Smetana's *Prodaná Nevêsta*
for the Metropolitan Opera, New York)

> *One afternoon the Band Conductor up on his stand*
> *Somehow lost his baton it flew out of his hand*
> *So I jumped in his place and conducted the band*
> *With mi little stick of Blackpool Rock!*
>   (GEORGE FORMBY)

Finale of ACT II. Though I resist
blurring the clarity of *hanba* (shame)
not wanting the least nuance to be missed
syllables run to rhubarb just the same . . .

Sorry, dad, you won't get that quatrain.
(I'd like to be the poet my father reads!)
It's all from you once saying on the train
how most of England's rhubarb came from Leeds.

Crochets and quavers, rhubarb silhouettes,
dark-shy sea-horse heads through waves of dung!
Rhubarb arias, duets, quartets
soar to precision from our common tongue.

The uke in the attic manhole once was yours!

Watch me on the rostrum wave my arms –

mi little stick of Leeds-grown *tusky* draws
galas of rhubarb from the MET-set palms.

1. *tusky*: the Leeds word for rhubarb.

The Ballad of Babelabour

*'This Babylonian confusion of words results from
their being the language of men who are going down'*
(BERTOLT BRECHT)

What ur-Sprache did the labour speak?
ur ur ur to t'master's Sprache
the hang-cur ur-grunt of the weak
the unrecorded urs of gobless workers

Their snaptins kept among their turds
they labour   eat and shit
with only grunts not proper words
raw material for t'poet

They're their own meat and their own dough
another block   another
a palace for the great Pharaoh
a prison for their brothers

Whatever name's carved on those stones
it's not the one who labours
an edifice of workers' bones
for one who wants no neighbours

Nimrod's nabobs like their bards
to laud the state's achievements
to eulogize his house of cards
and mourn the king's bereavements

The treasurer of Sprache's court
drops the bard his coppers
He knows that poets aren't his sort
but belong to the ur-crappers

Ur-crappers tongueless bardless nerks
your condition's shitty
no time for yer Collected Works
or modulated pity

but ur ur ur ur ur ur urs
sharpened into Sprache
revurlooshunairy vurse
uprising nacker starkers

by the time the bards have urd
and urd and urd and 𝔖prachered
the world's all been turned into *merde*
& Nimrod's Noah'sarkered

sailing t'shit in t'ship they urd at
no labour can embark her
try and you'll get guard-dog grrred at
the shitship's one class: 𝔖prache

Bards & labour left for dead
the siltworld's *neue neue*
bard   the HMV doghead
in that *negra negra* Goya.

(See the picture *A dog buried in the sand*
among the Black Paintings of Goya in the Prado.)

Book Ends

Baked the day she suddenly dropped dead
we chew it slowly that last apple pie.

Shocked into sleeplessness you're scared of bed.
We never could talk much, and now don't try.

You're like book ends, the pair of you, she'd say,
Hog that grate, say nothing, sit, sleep, stare . . .

The 'scholar' me, you, worn out on poor pay,
only our silence made us seem a pair.

Not as good for staring in, blue gas,
too regular each bud, each yellow spike.

A night you need my company to pass
and she not here to tell us we're alike!

Your life's all shattered into smithereens.

Back in our silences and sullen looks,
for all the Scotch we drink, what 's still between 's
not the thirty or so years, but books, books, books.

Turns

I thought it made me look more 'working class'
(as if a bit of chequered cloth could bridge that gap!)
I did a turn in it before the glass.
My mother said: *It suits you, your dad's cap.*
(She preferred me to wear suits and part my hair:
You're every bit as good as that lot are!)

All the pension queue came out to stare.
Dad was sprawled beside the postbox (still **VR**),
his cap turned inside up beside his head,
smudged **H A H** in purple Indian ink
and Brylcreem slicks displayed so folk might think
he wanted charity for dropping dead.

He never begged. For nowt! Death's reticence
crowns his life's, and *me*, I'm opening my trap
to busk the class that broke him for the pence
that splash like brackish tears into our cap.

Timer

Gold survives the fire that's hot enough
to make you ashes in a standard urn.
An envelope of coarse official buff
contains your wedding ring which wouldn't burn.

Dad told me I'd to tell them at St James's
the ring should go in the incinerator.
That 'eternity' inscribed with both their names is
his surety that they'd be together, 'later'.

I signed for the parcelled clothing as the son,
this cardy, apron, pants, bra, dress –

The clerk phoned down. *6-8-8-3-1* ?
Has she still her ring on? (Slight pause) *Yes*!

It's on my warm palm now, your burnished ring!

I feel your ashes, head, arms, breasts, womb, legs,
sift through its circle slowly, like that thing
you used to let me watch to time the eggs.

Long Distance

I

Your bed's got two wrong sides. Your life's all grouse.
I let your phone-call take its dismal course:

Ah can't stand it no more, this empty house!

Carrots choke us wi'out your mam's white sauce!

Them sweets you brought me, you can have 'em back.
Ah'm diabetic now. Got all the facts.
(The diabetes comes hard on the track
of two coronaries and cataracts.)

Ah've allus liked things sweet! But now ah push
food down mi throat! Ah'd sooner do wi'out.
And t'only reason now for beer's to flush
(so t'dietician said) mi kidneys out.

When I come round, they'll be laid out, the sweets,
Lifesavers, my father's New World treats,
still in the big brown bag, and only bought
rushing through JFK as a last thought.

II

Though my mother was already two years dead
Dad kept her slippers warming by the gas,
put hot water bottles her side of the bed
and still went to renew her transport pass.

You couldn't just drop in. You had to phone.
He'd put you off an hour to give him time
to clear away her things and look alone
as though his still raw love were such a crime.

He couldn't risk my blight of disbelief
though sure that very soon he'd hear her key
scrape in the rusted lock and end his grief.
He *knew* she'd just popped out to get the tea.

I believe life ends with death, and that is all.
You haven't both gone shopping; just the same,
in my new black leather phone book there's your name
and the disconnected number I still call.

Marked with D.

When the chilled dough of his flesh went in an oven
not unlike those he fuelled all his life,
I thought of his cataracts ablaze with Heaven
and radiant with the sight of his dead wife,
light streaming from his mouth to shape her name,
'not Florence and not Flo but always Florrie'.
I thought how his cold tongue burst into flame
but only literally, which makes me sorry,
sorry for his sake there's no Heaven to reach.
I get it all from Earth my daily bread
but he hungered for release from mortal speech
that kept him down, the tongue that weighed like lead.

The baker's man that no one will see rise
and England made to feel like some dull oaf
is smoke, enough to sting one person's eyes
and ash (not unlike flour) for one small loaf.

Self Justification

Me a poet! My daughter with maimed limb
became a more than tolerable sprinter.
And Uncle Joe. Impediment spurred him,
the worst stammerer I've known, to be a printer.

He handset type much faster than he spoke.
Those cruel consonants, ms, ps, and bs
on which his jaws and spirit almost broke
flicked into order with sadistic ease.

It seems right that Uncle Joe, 'b-buckshee
from the works', supplied those scribble pads
on which I stammered my first poetry
that made me seem a cissy to the lads.

Their aggro towards me, my need of them 's
what keeps my would-be mobile tongue still tied –

aggression, struggle, loss, blank printer's ems
by which all   eloquence   gets justified.

DOUGLAS DUNN

Men of Terry Street

They come in at night, leave in the early morning.
I hear their footsteps, the ticking of bicycle chains,
Sudden blasts of motorcycles, whimpering of vans.
Somehow I am either in bed, or the curtains are drawn.

This masculine invisibility makes gods of them,
A pantheon of boots and overalls.
But when you see them, home early from work
Or at their Sunday leisure, they are too tired

And bored to look long at comfortably.
It hurts to see their faces, too sad or too jovial.
They quicken their step at the smell of cooking,
They hold up their children and sing to them.

The Clothes Pit

The young women are obsessed with beauty.
Their old-fashioned sewing machines rattle in Terry Street.
They must keep up, they must keep up.

They wear teasing skirts and latest shoes,
Lush, impermanent coats, American cosmetics.
But they lack intellectual grooming.

In the culture of clothes and little philosophies,
They only have clothes. They do not need to be seen
Carrying a copy of *International Times*,

Or the Liverpool Poets, the wish to justify their looks
With things beyond themselves. They mix up colours,
And somehow they are often fat and unlovely.

They don't get high on pot, but get sick on cheap
Spanish Burgundy, or beer in rampant pubs,
And come home supported and kissed and bad-tempered.

But they have clothes, bright enough to show they dream
Of places other than this, an inarticulate paradise,
Eating exotic fowl in sunshine with courteous boys.

Three girls go down the street with the summer wind.
The litter of pop rhetoric blows down Terry Street,
Bounces past their feet, into their lives.

On Roofs of Terry Street

Television aerials, Chinese characters
In the lower sky, wave gently in the smoke.

Nest-building sparrows peck at moss,
Urban flora and fauna, soft, unscrupulous.

Rain drying on the slates shines sometimes.
A builder is repairing someone's leaking roof.

He kneels upright to rest his back.
His trowel catches the light and becomes precious.

A Removal from Terry Street

On a squeaking cart, they push the usual stuff,
A mattress, bed ends, cups, carpets, chairs,
Four paperback westerns. Two whistling youths
In surplus U.S. Army battle-jackets
Remove their sister's goods. Her husband
Follows, carrying on his shoulders the son
Whose mischief we are glad to see removed,
And pushing, of all things, a lawnmower.
There is no grass in Terry Street. The worms
Come up cracks in concrete yards in moonlight.
That man, I wish him well. I wish him grass.

Modern Love

It is summer, and we are in a house
That is not ours, sitting at a table
Enjoying minutes of a rented silence,
The upstairs people gone. The pigeons lull
To sleep the under-tens and invalids,
The tree shakes out its shadows to the grass,
The roses rove through the wilds of my neglect.
Our lives flap, and we have no hope of better
Happiness than this, not much to show for love
But how we are, or how this evening is,
Unpeopled, silent, and where we are alive
In a domestic love, seemingly alone,
All other lives worn down to trees and sunlight,
Looking forward to a visit from the cat.

In the Small Hotel

There they must live for ever, under soft lights,
The cheated at their favourite separate tables,
Inactive thirds of tender adulteries.

They stare into a light that is always evening,
Their eyes divided, as if distracted by
The ghost of something only one eye sees

Sleep-walking in plastic darkness
Around the night-clubs. They sit like chessmen
At their white round squares, waiting to be moved.

No one makes conversation. A hand
May absently arrange roses in a vase
Or wave away the leering gypsy fiddler.

Chefs please no one there and the waiters stamp
Untipped among customers too vague and lost
To ever think of coming back to commerce.

People we did not want or could not keep;
Someone did this to them, over and over
Wanting their unhappiness until it happened.

Over the dewy grass with a small suitcase
Love comes trotting and stops to hold on a shoe.
To go away with *her*! To drive the limousine

With contraceptives in the glove compartment
Beside the chocolates and packaged orchid
And find that new Arcadia replacing Hollywood!

Remote and amatory, that style of life
In which no one offends or intrudes.
They might as well live in their wardrobes.

Little Rich Rhapsody

For he has spent the summer in hotels
Of eight resorts. His miniature cocotte,
That handful of the mouthfuls, pleased him well.
Expensive, though; within a month he'd bought
More cunning clothes for her than used to pack
Mother's wardrobe, that sly adulteress
Who, when she died, left nothing but those clothes
In the Paris flat, the London flat, the villas,
Clothes on their wooden hangers, hanging slack
Just as she lived, he lives. Ah, happiness
Of hired cars and views of France, all those
Who stop at nothing and who thrill us
With rapid spendings, dissolutions through
Such finery of clothes of white and blue!

An Artist Waiting in a Country House

An artist waited in a country house
Set in a park, before a lake, and old.
He waited for a lady who had asked
To speak with him, for she had bought his works
And wished to make inquiries of his meaning
And his methods. From where he sat, he saw
The lady walking with her husband, who,
In riding boots, seemed something less than eager

To meet this person who was waiting in
A room that past munificence had warmed.
It seemed to be the finish of an argument
In which both he, the artist, and the lady,
Were subjects of a fanciful connivance
Or were accused of what they'd not intended.
He watched her husband kiss her on the cheek
And leave for somewhere else. He waited, sure
That her arrival was a matter of
A moment. He waited, waited, seated on
A sofa and the minutes passed, unlived,
More cinematic than anonymous.
He felt he'd walked into a private story.
Perhaps no one remembered where he was?
The room was one of fifty. They'd been built
When palaces were populous, and arts
Of masque and figure graced decisive eyes,
An architecture of success and wealth
In far, disreputable trades, or in
The purse of government, the secret gold
Of families. All artists know their pasts,
Those flung purses, when it was proper to
Ignore what now it is improper to
Ignore. Though does that matter much? He'd come
Because that lady asked, although he'd sensed
An obsoletion in the visit, an
Overdone propriety of interest
He felt was serious and entertaining,
Its charm undoubtedly, and why he'd come.
Let it happen, he wished aloud, waiting.
The minutes passed, unlived, and still. The room
Was furniture, an art, a heaven to
The fingers of the artisans who'd made it
While on the walls hung noted pictures by
Those other artists who had waited there,
The old originals. His gaze went out
Into the patterned cloth that shaped a chair
Into a fantasy of foliage,
And with it went the function of his eyes.
His eyes were where they should be, on his head;
And yet they were displaced. His mind thinks straight

Most of the time. Some days, to help him work,
Or justify, he bends his mind – just so –
On finding oppositions, those opposed
To what he knows but does not understand
Of what he does, believing it is art.
That day, he stared, so hard that sounds became
Factors of that patterned cloth, so deep
In colour where his gaze had taken him,
And not the slams of doors, or heels on floors,
Or voices raised as if forgetful of
Whatever urgency had made them raised;
Or children running on the crispy leaves;
Or that unskilful pianist playing tunes
Which his or her mistakes made beautiful.
Upon that chair, that lovely patterned cloth,
His gaze lay down. His mind and gaze were sly
And glozed by whispering an entrance to
The chair's amoral world, then went inside
To walk among unlikely foliage
Sensing delight, at one with the delights
Of a serenity, themselves serene, set free.
And loosed to pure inquiry they became
Spectators of release, spectators of
Themselves, himself. And it is terrible
To watch your own eyes watching you, intent
On clarity, from sockets that will twitch
To subtle judgements. By being gone from him,
He felt regret, and holding up his hand
To touch his eye, he touched its gift, a swim
Of body-water one had left behind,
A moistness on his eye, almost a drop.
Invisible fractures in everything.
An error in a pianist's luck. Barking.
The rattle of a dog-cart's wheels. Delights.

He looked behind him. The door had not opened.
When would it open? He was not sure.
He wanted it to open, and to smile,
On standing up, his hand stretched out
To shake the lady's hand and thank her for
Her acquisition of his several pictures.

Then he was sure. It would be always shut.
He would be there, sitting, waiting, always,
The woman always kissed upon her cheek,
Her husband turning, moving, to his stables
Or wherever or whatever or whoever
Was in this private story he had entered
Like a reader who was half-asleep, one eye
Reading as the other lived the story.
He waits, although that door will never open,
Unless he opens it, and walks away
And leaves the pictures hanging in the room
Focused on the sofa where he waited.

The woman, passing there, will stop, her hand
Will almost knock, almost reach the handle,
With the dry reds of the leaves falling
And children running on the dry, bright leaves,
In histories, like timetables, changes
Approximately chronicled as *happened*,
Something wrong in an unlucky autumn.
One moment for ever, and his gaze stuck
In the lovely patterned cloth of a chair,
So inadvertent, like his own mischance –
Heels on the wooden floors, doors slamming –
It might not be happening, though it is,
For what is melting on his cheek is proof,
The tear-drops of a melting eye, his gaze,
And round him stare the old originals.

Gardeners

England, Loamshire, 1789
*A gardener speaks, in the grounds of a
great house, to his Lordship*

Gardens, gardens, and we are gardeners . . .
Razored hedgerow, flowers, those planted trees
Whose avenues conduct a greater ease
Of shadow to your own and ladies' skins
And tilt this Nature to magnificence

And natural delight. But pardon us,
My Lord, if we reluctantly admit
Our horticulture not the whole of it,
Forgetting, that for you, this elegance
Is not our work, but your far tidier Sense.

Out of humiliation comes that sweet
Humility that does no good. We know
Our coarser artistries will make things grow.
Others design the craftsmanship we fashion
To please your topographical possession.
A small humiliation – Yes, we eat,
Our crops and passions tucked out of the view
Across a shire, the name of which is you,
Where every native creature runs upon
Hills, moors and meadows which your named eyes own.

Our eyes are nameless, generally turned
Towards the earth our fingers sift all day –
Your day, your earth, your eyes, wearing away
Not earth, eyes, days, but scouring, forcing down
What lives in us and which you cannot own.
One of us heard the earth cry out. It spurned
His hands. It threw stones in his face. We found
That man, my Lord, and he was mad. We bound
His hands together and we heard him say –
'Not me! Not me who cries!' We took away

That man – remember, Lord? – and then we turned,
Hearing your steward order us return,
His oaths, and how you treated us with scorn.
They call this grudge. Let me hear you admit
That in the country that's but half of it.
Townsmen will wonder, when your house was burned,
We did not burn your gardens and undo
What likes of us did for the likes of you;
We did not raze this garden that we made,
Although we hanged you somewhere in its shade.

The Come-on

'. . . the guardian, the king's son, who kept watch
over the gates of the garden in which I wanted to live.'
(ALBERT CAMUS)

To have watched the soul of my people
   Fingered by the callous
Enlivens the bitter ooze from my grudge.
   Mere seepage from 'background'
Takes over, blacking out what intellect
   Was nursed by school or book
Or had accrued by questioning the world.
   Enchanting, beloved texts
Searched in for a generous mandate for
   Believing who I am,
What I have lived and felt, might just as well
   Not exist when the vile
Come on with their 'coals in the bath' stories
   Or mock at your accent.
Even now I am an embarrassment
   To myself, my candour.
Listen now to the 'professional classes'
   Renewing claims to 'rights',
Possession of land, ownership of work,
   Decency of 'standards'.
In the bleep-bleep of versicles, leisure-novels,
   Black traffic of Oxbridge –
Books and bicycles, the bile of success –
   Men dressed in prunella
Utter credentials and their culture rules us,
   A culture of connivance,
Of 'authority', arts of bland recoveries.
   Where, then, is 'poetry'?
Brothers, they say that we have no culture.
   We are of the wrong world,
Our level is the popular, the media,
   The sensational columns,
Unless we enter through a narrow gate
   In a wall they have built
To join them in the 'disinterested tradition'

Of tea, of couplets dipped
In sherry and the decanted, portentous remark.
    Therefore, we'll deafen them
With the dull staccato of our typewriters.
    But do not misbehave –
Threats and thrashings won't work: we're outnumbered.
    Drink ale if you must still,
But learn to tell one good wine from another –
    Our honesty is cunning.
We will beat them with decorum, with manners,
    As sly as language is.
Take tea with the king's son at the seminars –
    He won't know what's happening.
Carry your learning as does the mimic his face.
    Know one knife from another.
You will lose heart: don't show it. Be patient;
    And sit on that high wall
In its obstacle glass chips, its barbed wire,
    Watching the gardeners.
One day we will leap down, into the garden,
    And open the gate – *wide, wide*.
We too shall be kings' sons and guardians,
    And then there will be no wall:
Our grudges will look quaint and terrible.

Empires

All the dead Imperia . . . They have gone
Taking their atlases and grand pianos.
They could not leave geography alone.
They conquered with the thistle and the rose.
To our forefathers it was right to raise
Their pretty flag at every foreign dawn
Then lower it at sunset in a haze
Of bugle-brass. They interfered with place,
Time, people, lives, and so to bed. They died
When it died. It had died before. It died
Before they did. They did not know it. Race,
Power, Trade, Fleet, a hundred regiments,
Postponed that final reckoning with pride,

Which was expensive. Counting up the cost
We plunder morals from the power they lost.
They ruined us. They conquered continents.
We filled their uniforms. We cruised the seas,
We worked their mines and made their histories.
You work, we rule, they said. We worked; they ruled.
They fooled the tenements. All men were fooled.
It still persists. It will be so, always.
Listen. An out-of-work apprentice plays
God Save the Queen on an Edwardian flute.
He is, but does not know it, destitute.

Remembering Lunch

Noticing from what they talk about, and how they stand, or walk,
That my friends have lost the ability or inclination to wander
Along the shores of an estuary or sea in contented solitude,
Disturbs me on the increasingly tedious subject of myself.
I long for more chances to walk along depopulated shores,
For more hours dedicated to fine discriminations of mud
As it shades from grey to silver or dries into soft pottery;
Discriminations of wind, sky, rough grasses and water-birds,
And, above all, to be well-dressed in tweeds and serviceable shoes
Although not like an inverted popinjay of the demented gentry
But as a schoolmaster of some reading and sensibility
Circa 1930 and up to his eccentric week-end pursuits, noticing,
Before the flood of specialists, the trace of lost peoples
In a partly eroded mound, marks in the earth, or this and that
Turned over with the aforementioned impermeable footwear.
Describing this to my strangely sophisticated companions
Is to observe them docket it for future reference in
A pigeon-hole of the mind labelled *Possible Satires*.
We are far gone in our own decay. I admit it freely,
Longing no more for even the wherewithal of decent sufficiency
Or whatever hypothetical brilliance makes it possible.
Whatever my friends long for, they no longer confess it
In the afternoon twilight of a long lunch in London
After that moment when the last carafe has been ordered.
Such delicate conversations of years gone by! You would think
Perceptions of this sort best left for approaching senility,

Especially as, in my case, I was not born ever to expect
To enjoy so long-drawn-out a lunchtime at steep prices
Among tolerant waiters resigned to our lasting presences
As if they sense a recapitulation by young men of young men
In that fine hour of Edwardian promise at the *Tour Eiffel*
Or expatriate Americans and Irishmen in 'twenties Paris.
It is pretty well standard among literary phenomena.
Whether in the Rome of Marcus Martialis or London ordinaries
Favoured by roaring playwrights and poets destined for
Future righteousness or a destructive addiction to sack,
Lunch, lunch is a unitary principle, as Balzac would tell you
And as any man of letters consulting his watch towards noon
Would undoubtedly endorse. Lunch is the business of capitals,
Whether in *L'Escargot Bienvenu, Gobbles,* or the cheap Italian
            joint.
Impoverished or priggish in the provinces, where talent is born,
The angry poets look towards London as to a sea of restaurants,
Cursing the overpriced establishments of where they live
And the small scatter of the like-minded not on speaking terms.
But even this pleasure has waned, and its sum of parts –
People shaking hands on the pavement, a couple entering
A taxi hailed in the London rain, the red tears on a bottle
And the absorbing conspiracies and asserted judgements
Of young men in the self-confident flush of their promise –
Its sum of parts no longer presents a street of epiphanies.
Too much now has been spoken, or published, or unpublished.
Manias without charm, cynicism without wit, and integrity
Lying around so long it has begun to stink, can be seen and heard.
To come down south from the country in a freshly pressed suit
Is no longer the exercise in youthful if gauche dignity
It was once in days of innocent enthusiasm without routine.
And so I look forward to my tweed-clad solitude, alone
Beside a widening estuary, the lighthoused island appearing
Where waves of the sea turmoil against the river's waters
Baring their salty teeth and roaring. And here I can stand –
Forgive me my fantasies as, Lord, I surely forgive you yours –
In a pretence of being a John Buchan of the underdog,
With my waistcoated breast puffed against the wind. What do
            they long for?
Propping up bars with them I can pretend to be as they are
Though I no longer know what they are thinking, if ever I did,

And, raising this civil if not entirely sympathetic interest
In what they feel, I know it contributes little to them,
Adding, as it does, to a change in myself they might not notice,
Causing me this pain as I realize the way I must change
Is to be different from friends I love and whose company –
When the last carafe was ordered, an outrageous remark spoken,
Or someone announced his plan for an innovating stanza
Or a new development in his crowded sex-life – whose company
Was a landmark in my paltry accumulation of knowledge.
Perhaps, after all, this not altogether satisfactory
Independence of mind and identity before larger notions
Is a better mess to be in, with a pocketful of bread and cheese,
My hipflask and the *Poésie* of Philippe Jaccottet,
Listening to the sea compose its urbane wilderness,
Although it is a cause for fear to notice that only my footprints
Litter this deserted beach with signs of human approach,
Each squelch of leather on mud complaining, *But where are you
    going?*

St Kilda's Parliament: 1879–1979
The photographer revisits his picture

On either side of a rock-paved lane,
Two files of men are standing barefooted,
Bearded, waistcoated, each with a tam-o'-shanter
On his head, and most with a set half-smile
That comes from their companionship with rock,
With soft mists, with rain, with roaring gales,
And from a diet of solan goose and eggs,
A diet of dulse and sloke and sea-tangle,
And ignorance of what a pig, a bee, a rat,
Or rabbit looks like, although they remember
The three apples brought here by a traveller
Five years ago, and have discussed them since.
And there are several dogs doing nothing
Who seem contemptuous of my camera,
And a woman who might not believe it
If she were told of the populous mainland.
A man sits on a bank by the door of his house,
Staring out to sea and at a small craft

Bobbing there, the little boat that brought me here,
Whose carpentry was slowly shaped by waves,
By a history of these northern waters.
Wise men or simpletons – it is hard to tell –
But in that way they almost look alike
You also see how each is individual,
Proud of his shyness and of his small life
On this outcast of the Hebrides
With his eyes full of weather and seabirds,
Fish, and whatever morsel he grows here.
Clear, too, is manhood, and how each man looks
Secure in the love of a woman who
Also knows the wisdom of the sun rising,
Of weather in the eyes like landmarks.
Fifty years before depopulation –
Before the boats came at their own request
To ease them from their dying babies –
It was easy, even then, to imagine
St Kilda return to its naked self,
Its archeology of hazelraw
And footprints stratified beneath the lichen.
See, how simple it all is, these toes
Playfully clutching the edge of a boulder.
It is a remote democracy, where men,
In manacles of place, outstare a sea
That rattles back its manacles of salt,
The moody jailer of the wild Atlantic.
         Traveller, tourist with your mind set on
Romantic Staffas and materials for
Winter conversations, if you should go there,
Landing at sunrise on its difficult shores,
On St Kilda you will surely hear Gaelic
Spoken softly like a poetry of ghosts
By those who never were contorted by
Hierarchies of cuisine and literacy.
You need only look at the faces of these men
Standing there like everybody's ancestors,
This flick of time I shuttered on a face.
Look at their sly, assuring mockery.
They are aware of what we are up to
With our internal explorations, our

Designs of affluence and education.
They know us so well, and are not jealous,
Whose be-all and end-all was an eternal
Casual husbandry upon a toehold
Of Europe, which, when failing, was not their fault.
You can see they have already prophesied
A day when survivors look across the stern
Of a departing vessel for the last time
At their gannet-shrouded cliffs, and the farewells
Of the St Kilda mouse and St Kilda wren
As they fall into the texts of specialists,
Ornithological visitors at the prow
Of a sullenly managed boat from the future.
They pose for ever outside their parliament,
Looking at me, as if they have grown from
Affection scattered across my own eyes.
And it is because of this that I, who took
This photograph in a year of many events –
The Zulu massacres, Tchaikovsky's opera –
Return to tell you this, and that after
My many photographs of distressed cities,
My portraits of successive elegants,
Of the emaciated dead, the lost empires,
Exploded fleets, and of the writhing flesh
Of dead civilians and commercial copulations,
That after so much of that larger franchise
It is to this island that I return.
Here I whittle time, like a dry stick,
From sunrise to sunset, among the groans
And sighings of a tongue I cannot speak,
Outside a parliament, looking at them,
As they, too, must always look at me
Looking through my apparatus at them
Looking. Benevolent, or malign? But who,
At this late stage, could tell, or think it worth it?
For I was there, and am, and I forget.

HUGO WILLIAMS

The Butcher

The butcher carves veal for two.
The cloudy, frail slices fall over his knife.

His face is hurt by the parting sinews
And he looks up with relief, laying it on the scales.

He is a rosy young man with white eyelashes
Like a bullock. He always serves me now.

I think he knows about my life. How we prefer
To eat in when it's cold. How someone

With a foreign accent can only cook veal.
He writes the price on the grease-proof packet

And hands it to me courteously. His smile
Is the official seal on my marriage.

The Couple Upstairs

Shoes instead of slippers down the stairs,
She ran out with her clothes

And the front door banged and I saw her
Walking crookedly, like naked, to a car.

She was not always with him up there,
And yet they seemed inviolate, like us,
Our loves in sympathy. Her going

Thrills and frightens us. We come awake
And talk excitedly about ourselves, like guests.

February the 20th Street

A coincidence must be
Part of a whole chain
Whose links are unknown to me.

I feel them round me
Everywhere I go: in queues,
In trains, under bridges,

People, or coincidences, flukes
Of logic which fail
Because of me, because

We move singly through streets,
The last of some sad species,
Pacing the floors of zoos,

Our luck homing forever
Backward through grasses
To the brink of another time.

Confessions of a Drifter
(after Tu Mu 803–852 A.D.)

I used to sell perfume in the New Towns.
I was popular in the saloons.
Professional women slept in my trailer.
Young salesgirls broke my heart. For ten years
I never went near our Main Office.

From shop to shop
And then from door to door I went
In a slowly diminishing circle of enchantment
With 'Soir de Paris' and 'Flower of the Orient'.

I used up all my good luck
Wetting the wrists of teenagers in bars
With 'English Rose' and 'Afro-Dizziac'
From giveaway dispensers.

From girl to girl
And then from bar to bar I went

In a slowly expanding circle
Of liquid replenishment.

I would park my trailer outside a door
So I could find it when I walked out of there,
Throwing back my shoulders at the night – a hero
To myself.

They knock on my window this morning. Too late
I wake out of my salesman's paradise,
The sperm drying on my thigh
And nothing but the name of a drifter in the New Towns.

Along These Lines

And so you cry for her, and the poem falls to the page
As if it knew all along that what we make of ourselves we take
From one another's hearts – tearing and shouting until we learn
How awkwardly, upstairs and behind shut doors we are born
Already owing interest on what we have borrowed from the
          world.

Holidays

We spread our things on the sand
In front of the hotel
And sit for hours on end
Like merchants under parasols
Our thoughts following the steamers
In convoy across the bay
While far away
Our holidays look back at us in surprise
From fishing boats and fairs
Or wherever they were going then
In their seaweed head-dresses.

Tides

The evening advances, then withdraws again
Leaving our cups and books like islands on the floor.
We are drifting you and I,
As far from one another as the young heroes
Of these two novels we have just laid down.
For that is happiness: to wander alone
Surrounded by the same moon, whose tides remind us of
      ourselves,
Our distances, and what we leave behind.
The lamp left on, the curtains letting in the light.
These things were promises. No doubt we will come back to
      them.

DEREK MAHON

Afterlives
for James Simmons

I

I wake in a dark flat
To the soft roar of the world.
Pigeons neck on the white
Roofs as I draw the curtains
And look out over London
Rain-fresh in the morning light.

This is our element, the bright
Reason on which we rely
For the long-term solutions.
The orators yap, and guns
Go off in a back-street;
But the faith does not die

That in our time these things
Will amaze the literate children
In their non-sectarian schools
And the dark places be
Ablaze with love and poetry
When the power of good prevails.

What middle-class cunts we are
To imagine for one second
That our privileged ideals
Are divine wisdom, and the dim
Forms that kneel at noon
In the city not ourselves.

2

I am going home by sea
For the first time in years.
Somebody thumbs a guitar
On the dark deck, while a gull
Dreams at the masthead,
The moon-splashed waves exult.

At dawn the ship trembles, turns
In a wide arc to back
Shuddering up the grey lough
Past lightship and buoy,
Slipway and dry dock
Where a naked bulb burns;

And I step ashore in a fine rain
To a city so changed
By five years of war
I scarcely recognize
The places I grew up in,
The faces that try to explain.

But the hills are still the same
Grey-blue above Belfast.
Perhaps if I'd stayed behind
And lived it bomb by bomb
I might have grown up at last
And learnt what is meant by home.

Ecclesiastes

God, you could grow to love it, God-fearing, God-
    chosen purist little puritan that,
for all your wiles and smiles, you are (the
    dank churches, the empty streets,
the shipyard silence, the tied-up swings) and
    shelter your cold heart from the heat
of the world, from woman-inquisition, from the
    bright eyes of children. Yes you could
wear black, drink water, nourish a fierce zeal
    with locusts and wild honey, and not
feel called upon to understand and forgive
    but only to speak with a bleak
afflatus, and love the January rains when they
    darken the dark doors and sink hard
into the Antrim hills, the bog meadows, the heaped
    graves of your fathers. Bury that red
bandana and stick, that banjo; this is your

country, close one eye and be king.
Your people await you, their heavy washing
    flaps for you in the housing estates –
a credulous people. God, you could do it, God
    help you, stand on a corner stiff
with rhetoric, promising nothing under the sun.

The Apotheosis of Tins

Having spent the night in a sewer of precognition,
    consoled by moon-glow, air-chuckle
        and the retarded
            pathos of mackerel,
we wake among shoe-laces and white wood
    to a raw wind and the cries of gulls.

Deprived of use, we are safe now
    from the historical nightmare
        and may give our attention at last
            to things of the spirit,
noticing for example the consanguinity
    of sand and stone,
        how they are thicker than water,
and the pebbles shorter than their shadows.

This is the terminal democracy
    of hatbox and crab,
        of hock and Windowlene.
            It is always rush-hour.
If we have learnt one thing from our desertion
    by the sour smudge on the horizon,
        from the erosion of labels,
            it is the value of self-definition.
No one, not even the poet
    whose shadow halts above us after
        dawn and before dark,
            will have our trust.
We resist your patronage, your reflective leisure.

Promoted artifacts by the dereliction
   of our creator, and greater now
      than the sum of his skills,
we shall be with you while there are beaches.

Imperishable by-products of the perishable will,
   we shall lie like skulls
      in the hands of soliloquists.
The longest queues in the science museum
   will form at our last homes
      saying, 'Think now,

      what an organic relation
   of art to life
in the dawn; what saintly
devotion to the notion of permanence
   in the flux of sensation
      and crisis, perhaps
         we can learn from them.'

Lives
for Seamus Heaney

First time out
I was a torc of gold
And wept tears of the sun.

That was fun
But they buried me
In the earth two thousand years

Till a labourer
Turned me up with a pick
In eighteen fifty-four

And sold me
For tea and sugar
In Newmarket-on-Fergus.

Once I was an oar
But stuck in the shore
To mark the place of a grave

When the lost ship
Sailed away. I thought
Of Ithaca, but soon decayed.

The time that I liked
Best was when
I was a bump of clay

In a Navaho rug,
Put there to mitigate
The too godlike

Perfection of that
Merely human artifact.
I served my maker well –

He lived long
To be struck down in
Tucson by an electric shock

The night the lights
Went out in Europe
Never to shine again.

So many lives,
So many things to remember!
I was a stone in Tibet,

A tongue of bark
At the heart of Africa
Growing darker and darker . . .

It all seems
A little unreal now,
Now that I am

An anthropologist
With my own
Credit card, dictaphone,

Army surplus boots,
And a whole boatload
Of photographic equipment.

I know too much
To be anything any more;
And if in the distant

Future someone
Thinks he has once been me
As I am today,

Let him revise
His insolent ontology
Or teach himself to pray.

A Refusal to Mourn

He lived in a small farmhouse
At the edge of a new estate.
The trim gardens crept
To his door, and car engines
Woke him before dawn
On dark winter mornings.

All day there was silence
In the bright house. The clock
Ticked on the kitchen shelf,
Cinders moved in the grate,
And a warm briar gurgled
When the old man talked to himself;

But the doorbell seldom rang
After the milkman went,
And if a coat-hanger
Knocked in an open wardrobe
That was a strange event
To be pondered on for hours

While the wind thrashed about
In the back garden, raking
The roof of the hen-house,
And swept clouds and gulls
Eastwards over the lough
With its flap of tiny sails.

Once a week he would visit
An old shipyard crony,
Inching down to the road
And the blue country bus

To sit and watch sun-dappled
Branches whacking the windows

While the long evening shed
Weak light in his empty house,
On the photographs of his dead
Wife and their six children
And the Missions to Seamen angel
In flight above the bed.

'I'm not long for this world'
Said he on our last evening,
'I'll not last the winter',
And grinned, straining to hear
Whatever reply I made;
And died the following year.

In time the astringent rain
Of those parts will clean
The words from his gravestone
In the crowded cemetery
That overlooks the sea
And his name be mud once again

And his boilers lie like tombs
In the mud of the sea bed
Till the next ice age comes
And the earth he inherited
Is gone like Neanderthal Man
And no records remain.

But the secret bred in the bone
On the dawn strand survives
In other times and lives,
Persisting for the unborn
Like a claw-print in concrete
After the bird has flown.

The Last of the Fire Kings

I want to be
Like the man who descends
At two milk churns

With a bulging
String bag and vanishes
Where the lane turns,

Or the man
Who drops at night
From a moving train

And strikes out over the fields
Where fireflies glow
Not knowing a word of the language.

Either way, I am
Through with history –
Who lives by the sword

Dies by the sword.
Last of the fire kings, I shall
Break with tradition and

Die by my own hand
Rather than perpetuate
The barbarous cycle.

Five years I have reigned
During which time
I have lain awake each night

And prowled by day
In the sacred grove
For fear of the usurper,

Perfecting my cold dream
Of a place out of time,
A palace of porcelain

Where the frugivorous
Inheritors recline
In their rich fabrics
Far from the sea.

But the fire-loving
People, rightly perhaps,
Will not countenance this,

Demanding that I inhabit,
Like them, a world of

Sirens, bin-lids
And bricked-up windows –

Not to release them
From the ancient curse
But to die their creature and be thankful.

The Banished Gods

Near the headwaters of the longest river
    There is a forest clearing,
        A dank, misty place
    Where light stands in columns
And birds sing with a noise like paper tearing.

Far from land, far from the trade routes,
    In an unbroken dream-time
        Of penguin and whale,
    The seas sigh to themselves
Reliving the days before the days of sail.

Where the wires end the moor seethes in silence,
    Scattered with scree, primroses,
        Feathers and faeces.
    It shelters the hawk and hears
In dreams the forlorn cries of lost species.

It is here that the banished gods are in hiding,
    Here they sit out the centuries
        In stone, water
    And the hearts of trees,
Lost in a reverie of their own natures –

Of zero-growth economics and seasonal change
    In a world without cars, computers
        Or chemical skies,
    Where thought is a fondling of stones
And wisdom a five-minute silence at moonrise.

Leaves

The prisoners of infinite choice
Have built their house
In a field below the woods
And are at peace.

It is autumn, and dead leaves
On their way to the river
Scratch like birds at the windows
Or tick on the road.

Somewhere there is an afterlife
Of dead leaves,
A stadium filled with an infinite
Rustling and sighing.

Somewhere in the heaven
Of lost futures
The lives we might have led
Have found their own fulfilment.

The Snow Party
for Louis Asekoff

Bashō, coming
To the city of Nagoya,
Is asked to a snow party.

There is a tinkling of china
And tea into china;
There are introductions.

Then everyone
Crowds to the window
To watch the falling snow.

Snow is falling on Nagoya
And farther south
On the tiles of Kyōto.

Eastward, beyond Irago,
It is falling
Like leaves on the cold sea.

Elsewhere they are burning
Witches and heretics
In the boiling squares,

Thousands have died since dawn
In the service
Of barbarous kings;

But there is silence
In the houses of Nagoya
And the hills of Ise.

A Disused Shed in Co. Wexford
for J. G. Farrell

> *Let them not forget us, the*
> *weak souls among the asphodels.*
> (SEFERIS, *Mythistorema*)

Even now there are places where a thought might grow –
Peruvian mines, worked out and abandoned
To a slow clock of condensation,
An echo trapped for ever, and a flutter
Of wildflowers in the lift-shaft,
Indian compounds where the wind dances
And a door bangs with diminished confidence,
Lime crevices behind rippling rainbarrels,
Dog corners for bone burials;
And in a disused shed in Co. Wexford,

Deep in the grounds of a burnt-out hotel,
Among the bathtubs and the washbasins
A thousand mushrooms crowd to a keyhole.
This is the one star in their firmament
Or frames a star within a star.
What should they do there but desire?
So many days beyond the rhododendrons
With the world waltzing in its bowl of cloud,
They have learnt patience and silence
Listening to the rooks querulous in the high wood.

They have been waiting for us in a foetor
Of vegetable sweat since civil war days,
Since the gravel-crunching, interminable departure
Of the expropriated mycologist.
He never came back, and light since then
Is a keyhole rusting gently after rain.
Spiders have spun, flies dusted to mildew
And once a day, perhaps, they have heard something –
A trickle of masonry, a shout from the blue
Or a lorry changing gear at the end of the lane.

There have been deaths, the pale flesh flaking
Into the earth that nourished it;
And nightmares, born of these and the grim
Dominion of stale air and rank moisture.
Those nearest the door grow strong –
'Elbow room! Elbow room!'
The rest, dim in a twilight of crumbling
Utensils and broken flower-pots, groaning
For their deliverance, have been so long
Expectant that there is left only the posture.

A half century, without visitors, in the dark –
Poor preparation for the cracking lock
And creak of hinges. Magi, moonmen,
Powdery prisoners of the old regime,
Web-throated, stalked like triffids, racked by drought
And insomnia, only the ghost of a scream
At the flash-bulb firing squad we wake them with
Shows there is life yet in their feverish forms.
Grown beyond nature now, soft food for worms,
They lift frail heads in gravity and good faith.

They are begging us, you see, in their wordless way,
To do something, to speak on their behalf
Or at least not to close the door again.
Lost people of Treblinka and Pompeii!
'Save us, save us,' they seem to say,
'Let the god not abandon us
Who have come so far in darkness and in pain.
We too had our lives to live.
You with your light meter and relaxed itinerary,
Let not our naive labours have been in vain!'

MICHAEL LONGLEY

Wounds

Here are two pictures from my father's head –
I have kept them like secrets until now:
First, the Ulster Division at the Somme
Going over the top with 'Fuck the Pope!'
'No Surrender!': a boy about to die,
Screaming 'Give 'em one for the Shankill!'
'Wilder than Gurkhas' were my father's words
Of admiration and bewilderment.
Next comes the London-Scottish padre
Resettling kilts with his swagger-stick,
With a stylish backhand and a prayer.
Over a landscape of dead buttocks
My father followed him for fifty years.
At last, a belated casualty,
He said – lead traces flaring till they hurt –
'I am dying for King and Country, slowly.'
I touched his hand, his thin head I touched.

Now, with military honours of a kind,
With his badges, his medals like rainbows,
His spinning compass, I bury beside him
Three teenage soldiers, bellies full of
Bullets and Irish beer, their flies undone.
A packet of Woodbines I throw in,
A lucifer, the Sacred Heart of Jesus
Paralysed as heavy guns put out
The night-light in a nursery for ever;
Also a bus-conductor's uniform –
He collapsed beside his carpet-slippers
Without a murmur, shot through the head
By a shivering boy who wandered in
Before they could turn the television down
Or tidy away the supper dishes.
To the children, to a bewildered wife,
I think 'Sorry Missus' was what he said.

Second Sight

My father's mother had the second sight.
Flanders began at the kitchen window –
The mangle rusting in No Man's Land, gas
Turning the antimacassars yellow
When it blew the wrong way from the salient.

In bandages, on crutches, reaching home
Before his letters, my father used to find
The front door on the latch, his bed airing.
'I watched my son going over the top.
He was carrying flowers out of the smoke.'

I have brought the *Pocket Guide to London*,
My *Map of the Underground*, an address –
A lover looking for somewhere to live,
A ghost among ghosts of aunts and uncles
Who crowd around me to give directions.

Where is my father's house, where my father?
If I could walk in on my grandmother
She'd see right through me and the hallway
And the miles of cloud and sky to Ireland.
'You have crossed the water to visit me.'

The Linen Workers

Christ's teeth ascended with him into heaven:
Through a cavity in one of his molars
The wind whistles: he is fastened for ever
By his exposed canines to a wintry sky.

I am blinded by the blaze of that smile
And by the memory of my father's false teeth
Brimming in their tumbler: they wore bubbles
And, outside of his body, a deadly grin.

When they massacred the ten linen workers
There fell on the road beside them spectacles,
Wallets, small change, and a set of dentures:
Blood, food particles, the bread, the wine.

Before I can bury my father once again
I must polish the spectacles, balance them
Upon his nose, fill his pockets with money
And into his dead mouth slip the set of teeth.

Swans Mating

Even now I wish that you had been there
Sitting beside me on the riverbank:
The cob and his pen sailing in rhythm
Until their small heads met and the final
Heraldic moment dissolved in ripples.

This was a marriage and a baptism,
A holding of breath, nearly a drowning,
Wings spread wide for balance where he trod,
Her feathers full of water and her neck
Under the water like a bar of light.

Love Poem

1

You define with your perfume
Infinitely shifting zones
And print in falls of talcum
The shadow of your foot.

2

Gossamers spun from your teeth,
So many light constructions
Describing as with wet wings
The gully under my tongue.

3

These wide migrations begin
In our seamier districts –
A slumdweller's pigeons
Released from creaking baskets.

Mayo Monologues

1. Brothers

I was a mother and a father to him
Once his pebble spectacles had turned cloudy
And his walk slowed to a chair by the fire.
Often I would come back from herding sheep
Or from the post office with our pensions
To find his darkness in darkness, the turf
Shifting ashes on to last flakes of light.
The room was made more silent by the flies
That circled the soup stains on his waistcoat.
The dog preferred to curl up under his hand
And raced ahead as soon as I neared the lane.
I read to him from one of his six books,
Thick pages dropping from the broken spines
Of *Westward Ho!* and *The Children's Reciter.*
Sometimes I pulled faces, and he didn't know,
Or I paraded naked in front of him
As though I was looking in a mirror.
Two neighbours came visiting after he died.
Mad for the learning, a character, they said
And awakened in me a pride of sorts.
I picture his hand when I stroke the dog,
His legs if I knock the kettle from the hearth.
It's his peculiar way of putting things
That fills in the spaces of Tullabaun.
The dregs stewed in the teapot remind me,
And wind creaming rainwater off the butt.

2. Housekeeper

She burst out laughing at the interview
Because he complained about his catheter.
I had come from the far end of the county
To nurse his lordship and, when he died, stayed on.
Every morning here I have been surprised
By the stream that flows in the wrong direction.
I miss a mountain at the kitchen window.
The house is shrinking slowly to a few rooms
Where for longer periods she hides away

And sits arguing with herself, a hare
That chews over its droppings in the form.
I have caught her reading my letters home,
Hiding Christmas cards behind the piano.
She makes jokes to the friendly gardener
About my whiskery chin, my varicose veins,
And tells me off like a child in front of him
Should my fingernails be stained or floury.
If I start to talk about going home
She pretends not to understand my accent.
The bell that summons the afternoon tray
Will soon be ringing out for a bed pan.
Furniture and ornaments seem to linger
And wait under dust sheets for her to die.
A last sheet will cover up her armchair
And the hare that melts into the mountainside
Will be white in winter and eating snow.

3. Self-heal

I wanted to teach him the names of flowers,
Self-heal and centaury; on the long acre
Where cattle never graze, bog asphodel.
Could I love someone so gone in the head
And, as they say, was I leading him on?
He'd slept in the cot until he was twelve
Because of his babyish ways, I suppose,
Or the lack of a bed: hadn't his father
Gambled away all but rushy pasture?
His skull seemed to be hammered like a wedge
Into his shoulders, and his back was hunched,
Which gave him an almost scholarly air.
But he couldn't remember the things I taught:
Each name would hover above its flower
Like a butterfly unable to alight.
That day I pulled a cuckoo-pint apart
To release the giddy insects from their cell.
Gently he slipped his hand between my thighs.
I wasn't frightened; and still I don't know why,
But I ran from him in tears to tell them.
I heard how every day for one whole week

He was flogged with a blackthorn, then tethered
In the hayfield. I might have been the cow
Whose tail he would later dock with shears,
And he the ram tangled in barbed wire
That he stoned to death when they set him free.

4. Arrest

The sergeant called me by my christian name
And waited an hour while I tidied up.
Not once did he mention why he had come
Or when and where he would take me away.
He just moved quietly from wall to wall
As I swept the floor towards the flagstones
And leaned brush and shovel, the broken tongs
Next to the spade and hoe I'd brought inside.
I emptied the half-used packet of tea
Into the caddy and dusted the lid.
In the leaky basin with its brown ring
I washed knife, fork, spoon, the two teacups
And the saucer that does for an ashtray.
I put back the stools where they usually stand,
Hung the towel to dry over one of them
And spread fresh newspapers on the table.
When I'd thrown the water from the basin
I turned it upside down on the turf stack,
Then I packed my shaving brush and razor
And smoored the fire as though I might return.
They have locked me up in the institute
Because I made love to the animals.
I'd sooner stand barefoot, without a cap
And take in my acres from a distance,
From the rocky hilltops or the seashore,
From the purgatory of the windy gaps.

FLEUR ADCOCK

The Ex-Queen among the Astronomers

They serve revolving saucer eyes,
dishes of stars; they wait upon
huge lenses hung aloft to frame
the slow procession of the skies.

They calculate, adjust, record,
watch transits, measure distances.
They carry pocket telescopes
to spy through when they walk abroad.

Spectra possess their eyes; they face
upwards, alert for meteorites,
cherishing little glassy worlds:
receptacles for outer space.

But she, exile, expelled, ex-queen,
swishes among the men of science
waiting for cloudy skies, for nights
when constellations can't be seen.

She wears the rings he let her keep;
she walks as she was taught to walk
for his approval, years ago.
His bitter features taunt her sleep.

And so when these have laid aside
their telescopes, when lids are closed
between machine and sky, she seeks
terrestrial bodies to bestride.

She plucks this one or that among
the astronomers, and is become
his canopy, his occultation;
she sucks at earlobe, penis, tongue

mouthing the tubes of flesh; her hair
crackles, her eyes are comet-sparks.
She brings the distant briefly close
above his dreamy abstract stare.

The Soho Hospital for Women

I

Strange room, from this angle:
white door open before me,
strange bed, mechanical hum, white lights.
There will be stranger rooms to come.

As I almost slept I saw the deep flower opening
and leaned over into it, gratefully.
It swimmingly closed in my face. I was not ready.
It was not death, it was acceptance.

*

Our thin patient cat died purring,
her small triangular head tilted back,
the nurse's fingers caressing her throat,
my hand on her shrunken spine; the quick needle.

That was the second death by cancer.
The first is not for me to speak of.
It was telephone calls and brave letters
and a friend's hand bleeding under the coffin.

*

Doctor, I am not afraid of a word.
But neither do I wish to embrace that visitor,
to engulf it as Hine-Nui-te-Po
engulfed Maui; that would be the way of it.

And she was the winner there: her womb crushed him.
Goddesses can do these things.
But I have admitted the gloved hands and the speculum
and must part my ordinary legs to the surgeon's knife.

II

Nellie has only one breast
ample enough to make several.
Her quilted dressing-gown softens
to semi-doubtful this imbalance
and there's no starched vanity
in our abundant ward-mother:

her silvery hair's in braids, her slippers
loll, her weathered smile holds true.
When she dresses up in her black
with her glittering marcasite brooch on
to go for the weekly radium treatment
she's the bright star of the taxi-party –
whatever may be growing under her ribs.

                    *

Doris hardly smokes in the ward –
and hardly eats more than a dreamy spoonful –
but the corridors and bathrooms
reek of her Players Number 10,
and the drug-trolley pauses
for long minutes by her bed.
Each week for the taxi-outing
she puts on her skirt again
and has to pin the slack waistband
more tightly over her scarlet sweater.
Her face, a white shadow through smoked glass,
lets Soho display itself unregarded.

                    *

Third in the car is Mrs Golding
who never smiles. And why should she?

III

The senior consultant on his rounds
murmurs in so subdued a voice
to the students marshalled behind
that they gather in, forming a cell,
a cluster, a rosette around him
as he stands at the foot of my bed
going through my notes with them,
half-audibly instructive, grave.

The slight ache as I strain forward
to listen still seems imagined.

Then he turns his practised smile on me:
'How are you this morning?' 'Fine,
very well, thank you.' I smile too.

And possibly all that murmurs within me
is the slow dissolving of stitches.

IV

I am out in the supermarket choosing –
this very afternoon, this day –
picking up tomatoes, cheese, bread,

things I want and shall be using
to make myself a meal, while they
eat their stodgy suppers in bed:

Janet with her big freckled breasts,
her prim Scots voice, her one friend,
and never in hospital before,

who came in to have a few tests
and now can't see where they'll end;
and Coral in the bed by the door

who whimpered and gasped behind a screen
with nurses to and fro all night
and far too much of the day;

pallid, bewildered, nineteen.
And Mary, who will be all right
but gradually. And Alice, who may.

Whereas I stand almost intact,
giddy with freedom, not with pain.
I lift my light basket, observing

how little I needed in fact;
and move to the checkout, to the rain,
to the lights and the long street curving.

A Surprise in the Peninsula

When I came in that night I found
the skin of a dog stretched flat and
nailed upon my wall between the
two windows. It seemed freshly killed –

there was blood at the edges. Not
my dog: I have never owned one,
I rather dislike them. (Perhaps
whoever did it knew that.) It
was a light brown dog, with smooth hair;
no head, but the tail still remained.
On the flat surface of the pelt
was branded the outline of the
peninsula, singed in thick black
strokes into the fur: a coarse map.
The position of the town was
marked by a bullet-hole; it went
right through the wall. I placed my eye
to it, and could see the dark trees
outside the house, flecked with moonlight.
I locked the door then, and sat up
all night, drinking small cups of the
bitter local coffee. A dog
would have been useful, I thought, for
protection. But perhaps the one
I had been given performed that
function; for no one came that night,
nor for three more. On the fourth day
it was time to leave. The dog-skin
still hung on the wall, stiff and dry
by now, the flies and the smell gone.
Could it, I wondered, have been meant
not as a warning, but a gift?
And, scarcely shuddering, I drew
the nails out and took it with me.

A Walk in the Snow

Neighbours lent her a tall feathery dog
to make her expedition seem natural.
She couldn't really fancy a walk alone,
drawn though she was to the shawled whiteness,
the flung drifts of wool. She was not a walker.
Her winter pleasures were in firelit rooms –
entertaining friends with inventive dishes

or with sherry, conversation, palm-reading:
'You've suffered' she'd say. 'Of course, life is suffering . . .'
holding a wrist with her little puffy hand
older than her face. She was writing a novel.
But today there was the common smothered in snow,
blanked-out, white as meringue, the paths gone:
a few mounds of bracken spikily veiled
and the rest smooth succulence. They pocked it,
she and the dog; they wrote on it with their feet –
her suede boots, his bright flurrying paws.
It was their snow, and they took it.

                        That evening
the poltergeist, the switcher-on of lights
and conjuror with ashtrays, was absent.
The house lay mute. She hesitated a moment
at bedtime before the Valium bottle;
then, to be on the safe side, took her usual;
and swam into a deep snowy sleep
where a lodge (was it?) and men in fur hats,
and the galloping . . . and something about . . .

Against Coupling

I write in praise of the solitary act:
of not feeling a trespassing tongue
forced into one's mouth, one's breath
smothered, nipples crushed against the
ribcage, and that metallic tingling
in the chin set off by a certain odd nerve:

unpleasure. Just to avoid those eyes would help –
such eyes as a young girl draws life from,
listening to the vegetal
rustle within her, as his gaze
stirs polypal fronds in the obscure
sea-bed of her body, and her own eyes blur.

There is much to be said for abandoning
this no longer novel exercise –
for not 'participating in

a total experience' – when
one feels like the lady in Leeds who
had seen *The Sound of Music* eighty-six times;

or more, perhaps, like the school drama mistress
producing *A Midsummer Night's Dream*
for the seventh year running, with
yet another cast from 5B.
Pyramus and Thisbe are dead, but
the hole in the wall can still be troublesome.

I advise you, then, to embrace it without
encumbrance. No need to set the scene,
dress up (or undress), make speeches.
Five minutes of solitude are
enough – in the bath, or to fill
that gap between the Sunday papers and lunch.

ANNE STEVENSON

The Marriage

They will fit, she thinks,
but only if her backbone
cuts exactly into his rib cage,
and only if his knees
dock exactly under her knees
and all four
agree on a common angle.

All would be well
if only
they could face each other.

Even as it is
there are compensations
for having to meet
nose to neck
chest to scapula
groin to rump
when they sleep.

They look, at least,
as if they were going
in the same direction.

Utah

Somewhere nowhere in Utah, a boy by the roadside,
gun in his hand, and the rare dumb hard tears flowing.
Beside him, the greyheaded man has let one arm slide
awkwardly over his shoulder, is talking and pointing
at whatever it is, dead, in the dust on the ground.

By the old parked Chevy, two women, talking and watching.
Their skirts flag forward. Bandannas twist with their hair.
Around them some sheep and a fence and the sagebrush burning
and burning with its blue flame. In the distance, where
mountains are clouds, lightning, but no rain.

from Correspondences

A Daughter's Difficulties as a Wife:
Mrs Reuben Chandler to her mother in New Orleans

September 3, 1840   Cincinnati, Ohio

Now that I've been married for almost four weeks, Mama,
   I'd better drop you and Papa dear a line.
      I guess I'm fine.

Ruby has promised to take me to the Lexington
   buggy races Tuesday, if the weather cools.
      So far we've not been out much.

Just stayed here stifling in hot Cincinnati.
   Clothes almost melt me, Mama, so I've not got out
      my lovely red velvet-and-silk pelisse yet,

or that sweet little lambskin coat with the fur hood.
   The sheets look elegant!
      I adore the pink monogram on the turnover

with exactly the same pattern on the pillowcases!
   Darlings!
      How I wish you could breeze in and admire them!

And the table linen,
   and the bone china,
      and the grand silver candlesticks,

and especially those
   long-stemmed Venetian wine glasses
      with the silver rims.

My, didn't your little daughter
   play the queen the other day
      serving dinner to a whole bevy of bachelors!

To tell the truth, Mama,
   Reuben was a silly to ask them,
      just imagine me, tiny wee me,

hostess to fourteen dragons
 and famished monsters,
   doing battle with fuming pipes and flying plugs.

Poor Rube!
 He doesn't chew and hardly ever smokes.
   He must have felt out of place.

I was frantic, naturally,
 for fear of wine stains and
   tobacco juice on the table cloth,

so I set Agatha to dart in and dab with a towel,
 and told Sue in the kitchen, to brew up some coffee
   quick, before they began speechmaking.

But it was no use.
 They would put me up on a chair after the ices,
   and one of them – Big Tom they call him –

(runs a sizable drygoods business here)
 well, this Tom pulled off my shoe,
   tried to drink wine out of it while

I was dying of laughter,
 and Tom was laughing too, when suddenly
   I slipped, and fell on the Flemish decanter!

It broke.
 Such a terrible pity.
   And so funny at the same time.

I must admit the boys were bricks,
 carrying the tablecloth out to the kitchen,
   holding it out while I

poured hot water from a height,
 just as you always said to.
   Everything would have been all right.

The party could have gone on.
 Then Reuben had to nose in and spoil things,
   sending me to bed!

So the boys went off, kind of sheepish.

Later Reuben said I had disgraced us
    and where was I brought up anyway,
        to behave like a bar maid!

But it wasn't my fault, Mama.
    They were his friends. He invited them.
        I like to give men a good time!

I'm writing this in bed because
    my head thumps and drums every time I move
        and I'm so dog tired!

The only time I sleep is in the morning
    when Reuben has left for the office.
        Which brings up a *delicate* subject, Mama.

I've been thinking and thinking,
    wondering whether I'll *ever* succeed in being
        the tender, devoted little wife you wanted me to be.

Because . . . oh, Mama,
    why didn't you tell me or warn me before I was married
        that a wife is expected to do it *every night*!

But how could we have guessed?
    Ruby came courting so cool and fine and polite,
        while beneath that gentlemanly, educated exterior . . .

well! I don't like to worry you, Mama.
    You know what men are like!
        I remember you said once the dears couldn't help it.

I try to be brave.
    But if you *did* have a chance to speak to Papa,
        mightn't you ask him to slip a word,

sort of man to man to Reuben . . .
    about how delicate I am
        and how sick I am every month,

not one of those cows
  who can be used and used?
    Someone's at the door.

I forgot,
  I asked Fanny Daniels to come up this morning
    to help fix a trim for my hat.

I'll have to hustle!
  Give all my love to dear Spooky and Cookie.
  How I miss them, the doggy darlings!

Oceans of hugs and kisses for you, too,
  and for precious Papa,

    From your suffering and loving daughter,

      Marianne

A Love Letter:
Ruth Arbeiter to Major Paul Maxwell

September 3, 1945   Clearfield, Vermont

Dearest,

You must know that I think of you continually,
often entering unexpectedly
that brighter isolate planet where we two live.
Which resembles this earth – its air,
grass, houses, beds, laundry, things to eat –
except that it is articulate,
the accessory, understanding, speaking of
where we are born and love and
move together continually.

Departures are dreams of home,
returns to bodies and minds we're in the habit of.
And what are these terrible things
they are taking for granted? Air and grass,
houses and beds, laundry and things to eat –
so little clarity, so little space between them;
a crowd of distractions to be

bought and done and arranged for,
drugs for the surely incurable pain of
living misunderstood among many who love you.

One evening not long ago
I walked to the high flat stone where,
as children, we used to lie in wait
for the constellations. It was dusk and hazy,
the hills, soft layers of differentiated shadow
thick with the scraping of crickets, or katydids,
or whatever you call those shrill unquenchable insects,
sawing their way through night after summer night.
Seated on the stone,
straining into the distance,
it was strangely as if I were
seeing through sound. As if an intensity,
a nagging around me, somehow *became* the mist –
the hills, too, breathing quietly, the sun
quietly falling, disappearing through gauze.

Such seeings have occurred frequently
since we were together. Your quality of perceiving,
a way through, perhaps, or out of, this
damaging anguish. As when we looked down –
you remember that day – into the grassy horse pool
where one bull frog and one crimson maple leaf
quietly brought our hands together.

Dearest, what more can I say?
Here, among my chores and my children.
Mine and my husband's children. So many friends.
And in between, these incredible perspectives,
openings entirely ours in the eddying numbness
where, as you know, I am waiting for you
continually.
                    Ruth

Respectable House

Worth keeping your foot in the door.
Worth letting the lamplight stripe your shoe
and escape in the dark behind you.

Worth the candle-width of a velvet floor,
the swell of a stair, a tinkle of glasses,
and overheard – rising and flaring – those fortunate voices.

Push open the door. More. And a little more.
You seem to be welcome. You can't help stepping inside.
You see how light and its residents have lied.

You see what the gun on the table has to be used for.

With my Sons at Boarhills

Gulls think it is for them
that the wormy sand rises,
brooding on its few rights,
losing its war with water.

The mussel flats ooze out,
and now the barnacled, embossed
stacked rocks are pedestals for strangers,
for my own strange sons,
scraping in the pool,
imperilling their pure reflections.

Their bodies are less beautiful than
blue heaven's pleiades of herring gulls,
or gannets, or that sloop's sail
sawtoothing the sea as if its
scenery were out of date, as if its
photographs had all been taken:
two boys left naked in a sloughed off summer,
skins and articulate backbones,
fossils for scrapbook or cluttered mantelpiece.

If you look now, quickly and askance,
you can see how the camera's eye
perfected what was motion and chance before
it clicked on this day and childhood snapshot,

scarcely seen beside
hunched rugby stripes and ugly uniforms –
shy, familiar grins in a waste of faces.

My knee joints ache and crack
as I kneel to my room's fire, feeding it.
Steam wreathes from my teacup, clouding
the graduate, the lieutenant, the weddings,
the significant man of letters, the politician
smiling from his short victory . . .

Faces I washed and scolded, only
watched as my each child laboured from his own womb,
bringing forth, without me, men who must
call me mother, love or reassess me
as their barest needs dictate, return
dreaming, rarely to this saltpool in memory,
naked on a morning full of see-through jellyfish,
with the tide out and the gulls out
grazing on healed beaches,
while sea-thrift blazes by the dry path,
and the sail stops cutting the water to pieces
and heads for some named port inland.

Their voices return like footprints over the sandflats,
permanent, impermanent, salt and sensuous
as the sea is, in its frame, its myth.

North Sea off Carnoustie
for Jean Rubens

You know it by the northern look of the shore,
by the salt-worried faces,
by an absence of trees, and abundance of lighthouses.
It's a serious ocean.

Along marram-scarred, sandbitten margins
wired roofs straggle out to where
a cold little holiday fair
has floated in and pitched itself
safely near the prairie of the golf course.
Coloured lights are sunk deep into the solid wind,

but all they've caught is a pair of lovers
and three silly boys.
Everyone else has a dog.
Or a room to get to.

The smells are of fish and of sewage and cut grass.
Oystercatchers, doubtful of habitation,
clamour 'weep, weep, weep' as they fuss over
scummy black rocks the tide leaves for them.

The sea is as near as we come to another world.

But there in your stony and windswept garden
a blackbird is confirming the grip of the land.
'You, you,' he murmurs, dark purple in his voice.

And now in far quarters of the horizon
lighthouses are awake, sending messages –
invitations to the landlocked,
warnings to the experienced,
but to anyone returning from the planet ocean,
candles in the windows of a safe earth.

JAMES FENTON

The Kingfisher's Boxing Gloves
(*le martin-pêcheur et ses gants bourrés*)
from the French

The walrus stretches forth a wrinkled hand.
The petrel winks a dull, mascaraed eye.
Dusk comes softly, treading along the sand.
Along the wet spar and the hornbeam sky
Night is secreted in the orbit's gland.
The alligator yawns and heaves a sigh.
Along its teeth, black as an upright grand,
The mastik bird performs its dentistry.

So much sand that a man ere night becomes
A perfect hourglass. Out among the dunes
They stretch the vellum on the savage drums.
The hotel bar is hushed. The bootboy croons
Softly. The manager completes his sums
And shuts the register. The end of June's
The end of his season. The song he hums
Clashes at midnight with the savage tunes.

It is the marram grass, the marram grass
That soughs beneath my balcony all night,
That claws the webbed feet of the beasts that pass,
That irritates the nostrils till they fight.
Fed up with sand, tired of treading on glass,
I take the coach and leave tomorrow night
For colder, milder northern climes, alas
With friends of whom I cannot bear the sight.

The diamond cutter working for de Beers,
The lady with the yashmak from Zem-Zem,
The tattooed man, the girl with jutting ears,
The lovely bishop with the kiss-worn gem,
That pair of cataleptic engineers,
I throw out pontoon bridges to meet them
And take on new, funicular veneers,
Thanking my stars that this is just pro tem.

The cicerone is unknown to flap,
The sort of chap who never makes a slip.
He can provide the only useful map.
He tells the men how much and when to tip.
He buys the sort of rope that will not snap
On the descent. He tells you where to grip.
That it's the thirteenth step that springs the trap.
That smugglers sweat along the upper lip.

For this, much thanks. The way is often steep
And rust betrays the pitons of the blind.
The pollen count is up. The folding jeep
Sticks in the mud and must be left behind.
An engineer is murdered in his sleep.
The bishop owns a gun, owns up, is fined.
The other engineer begins to weep
And finally admits, he's changed his mind.

'So soon!' the bishop cries, 'Come off it, Keith.
It's several hours too early to be scared.
The breasts are all behind us and the see-th-
rough skirts long past, their trials and dangers dared.'
(Up flies the kingfisher. It bares its teeth,
With orange laughter lines and nostrils flared.
Its long crow's feet are spreading out beneath.)
'I would have stayed if I had thought you cared.

'I would have been the party's life and soul,
But all you wanted was a bed of nails.
I would have chopped the logs and fetched the coal,
But all you lived on was the light that fails.
I would have muscled in with bone-and-roll,
But all your victuals came from fagged-out quails.
You trundle on and fossick out your goal.
But as for me, I'm through. I've furled my sails.'

His LEM is waiting at the station
To take him to the mountains of the moon.
On board he hears the countdown with elation,
Is horrified to see his mother swoon
And turn into a dim, distant relation

He sees his world become a macaroon.
'Quite a small step for our civilization –
Not at all bad for a legless baboon.'

We track the craft with cynical defiance,
Raising our damp proboscises to sniff
At such a flight, such pitiful reliance
Upon the parabolic hippogriff.
The module vanishes. Blinded by science.
We camp along the edges of the cliff.
Who slip between the sheets at night with giants
Will wake to pillow dew and morning stiff.

Under the glass dome all its feathers wilt.
The kingfisher grows tetchy and looks bored.
Beneath the cliffs the dawn spreads miles of silt
And lug-worm castings where the breakers roared
Last night. The tattooed man beneath his quilt
Fondles his tattooed limbs. The cutter's hoard
Supports his head, locked in its custom-built
Toledo-steel-bound chest. He grasps his sword.

All fast asleep. The kingfisher and I
Exchange a soulful look, thinking of Home.
The shovellers home shrieking through the sky.
The kingfisher coughs twice and shakes its comb.
'Don't bite your nails so!' But the bird is sly,
Stares at the red horizon where the foam
Curls like a lip, and weeps 'Ah, let us fly!'
Nettled, I raise my arm – and break the dome.

A Vacant Possession

In a short time we shall have cleared the gazebo.
Look how you can scrape the weeds from the paving stones
With a single motion of the foot. Paths lead down
Past formal lawns, orchards, notional guinea-fowl
To where the house is entirely obscured from view.

And there are gravel drives beneath the elm-tree walks
On whose aquarium green the changing weather
Casts no shadow. Urns pour their flowers out beside
A weathered Atlas with the whole world to support.
Look, it is now night and there are lights in the trees.

The difficult guest is questioning his rival.
He is pacing up and down while she leans against
A mossy water-butt in which, could we see them,
Innumerable forms of life are uncurving.
She is bravely not being hurt by his manner

Of which they have warned her. He taps his cigarette
And brusquely changes the subject. He remembers
Something said earlier which she did not really mean.
Nonsense – she did mean it. Now he is satisfied.
She has bitten the quick of her thumb-nail, which bleeds.

What shall we do the next day? The valley alters.
You set out from the village and the road turns around.
So that, in an hour, behind a clump of oak-trees,
With a long whitewashed wall and a low red-tiled roof
Peaceful, unevenly they appear again.

The square, the café seats, the doorways are empty
And the long grey balconies stretch out on all sides.
Time for an interlude, evening in the country,
With distant cowbells providing the angelus.
But we are interrupted by the latest post.

'Of course you will never understand. How could you?
You had everything. Everything always went well
For you. If there was a court at which I could sue you
I should take you for every memory you have.
No doubt you are insured against your murdered friends.'

Or: 'We see very little of Hester these days.
Why don't you come home? Your room is as you left it.
I went in yesterday, looking for notepaper,
And – do you know – the noose is still over the bed!
Archie says he will bring it out to you this summer.'

On warm spring afternoons, seated in the orchard,
The smocked, serious students develop grave doubts
About Pascal's wager. Monsieur le Curé stays
Chatting till midnight over the porcelain stove.
The last of his nine proofs lies smouldering in the grate.

I have set up my desk in an old dressing-room
So that the shadow of the fig-tree will be cast
On this page. At night, above the mountain opposite,
The beam of approaching cars is seen in the sky.
And now a slamming door and voices in the hall,

Scraping suitcases and laughter. Shall I go down?
I hear my name called, peer over the banister
And remember something I left in my bedroom.
What can it have been? The window is wide open.
The curtains move. The light sways. The cold sets in.

A German Requiem

It is not what they built. It is what they knocked down.
It is not the houses. It is the spaces between the houses.
It is not the streets that exist. It is the streets that no longer exist.
It is not your memories which haunt you.
It is not what you have written down.
It is what you have forgotten, what you must forget.
What you must go on forgetting all your life.
And with any luck oblivion should discover a ritual.
You will find out that you are not alone in the enterprise.
Yesterday the very furniture seemed to reproach you.
Today you take your place in the Widows' Shuttle.

    *

The bus is waiting at the southern gate
To take you to the city of your ancestors
Which stands on the hill opposite, with gleaming pediments,
As vivid as this charming square, your home.
Are you shy? You should be. It is almost like a wedding,
The way you clasp your flowers and give a little tug at your veil. Oh,
The hideous bridesmaids, it is natural that you should resent them

Just a little, on this first day.
But that will pass, and the cemetery is not far.
Here comes the driver, flicking a toothpick into the gutter,
His tongue still searching between his teeth.
See, he has not noticed you. No one has noticed you.
It will pass, young lady, it will pass.

*

How comforting it is, once or twice a year,
To get together and forget the old times.
As on those special days, ladies and gentlemen,
When the boiled shirts gather at the graveside
And a leering waistcoat approaches the rostrum.
It is like a solemn pact between the survivors.
The mayor has signed it on behalf of the freemasonry.
The priest has sealed it on behalf of all the rest.
Nothing more need be said, and it is better that way –

*

The better for the widow, that she should not live in fear of
        surprise,
The better for the young man, that he should move at liberty
        between the armchairs,
The better that these bent figures who flutter among the graves
Tending the nightlights and replacing the chrysanthemums
Are not ghosts,
That they shall go home.
The bus is waiting, and on the upper terraces
The workmen are dismantling the houses of the dead.

*

But when so many had died, so many and at such speed,
There were no cities waiting for the victims.
They unscrewed the name-plates from the shattered doorways
And carried them away with the coffins.
So the squares and parks were filled with the eloquence of
        young cemeteries:
The smell of fresh earth, the improvised crosses
And all the impossible directions in brass and enamel.

*

'Doctor Gliedschirm, skin specialist, surgeries 14–16 hours or
        by appointment.'

Professor Sargnagel was buried with four degrees, two associate
        memberships
And instructions to tradesmen to use the back entrance.
Your uncle's grave informed you that he lived on the third floor,
        left.
You were asked please to ring, and he would come down in the
        lift
To which one needed a key . . .

        *

Would come down, would ever come down
With a smile like thin gruel, and never too much to say.
How he shrank through the years.
How you towered over him in the narrow cage.
How he shrinks now . . .

        *

But come. Grief must have its term? Guilt too, then.
And it seems there is no limit to the resourcefulness of
        recollection.
So that a man might say and think:
When the world was at its darkest,
When the black wings passed over the rooftops
(And who can divine His purposes?) even then
There was always, always a fire in this hearth.
You see this cupboard? A priest-hole!
And in that lumber-room whole generations have been housed
        and fed.
Oh, if I were to begin, if I were to begin to tell you
The half, the quarter, a mere smattering of what we went
        through!

        *

His wife nods, and a secret smile,
Like a breeze with enough strength to carry one dry leaf
Over two pavingstones, passes from chair to chair.
Even the inquirer is charmed.
He forgets to pursue the point.
It is not what he wants to know.
It is what he wants not to know.
It is not what they say.
It is what they do not say.

In a Notebook

There was a river overhung with trees
With wooden houses built along its shallows
From which the morning sun drew up a haze
And the gyrations of the early swallows
Paid no attention to the gentle breeze
Which spoke discreetly from the weeping willows.
There was a jetty by the forest clearing
Where a small boat was tugging at its mooring.

And night still lingered underneath the eaves.
In the dark houseboats families were stirring
And Chinese soup was cooked on charcoal stoves.
Then one by one there came into the clearing
Mothers and daughters bowed beneath their sheaves.
The silent children gathered round me staring
And the shy soldiers setting out for battle
Asked for a cigarette and laughed a little.

From low canoes old men laid out their nets
While on the bank young boys with lines were fishing.
The wicker traps were drawn up by their floats.
The girls stood waist-deep in the river washing
Or tossed the day's rice on enamel plates
And I sat drinking bitter coffee wishing
The tide would turn to bring me to my senses
After the pleasant war and the evasive answers.

There was a river overhung with trees.
The girls stood waist-deep in the river washing,
And night still lingered underneath the eaves
While on the bank young boys with lines were fishing.
Mothers and daughters bowed beneath their sheaves
While I sat drinking bitter coffee wishing –
And the tide turned and brought me to my senses.
The pleasant war brought the unpleasant answers:

The villages are burnt, the cities void;
The morning light has left the river view;
The distant followers have been dismayed;
And I'm afraid, reading this passage now,
That everything I knew has been destroyed

By those whom I admired but never knew;
The laughing soldiers fought to their defeat
And I'm afraid most of my friends are dead.

Nest of Vampires

From the bare planks the reflected sun lights up
The white squares on the wall released by pictures
Depicting Tivoli, an imperial
    Family in its humiliation,
        Cows up to their knees in a cool stream

And a man in Dovedale reaching for a branch.
What fell behind the desk, what levelled the leg
Of the card-table, what had been presumed lost
    Has been found. In that chest there was a box
        Containing a piece of white coral,

A silver cigar-cutter shaped like a pike,
A chipping taken from the Great Pyramid
And a tribal fetish stolen during war:
    'This is something shameful. You must never
        Mention its existence to a soul.'

But there was so much one should never mention.
If one day those three turbaned Sikhs were announced
To have taken lodgings down in the village
    Or if, walking at evening through the grounds,
        Where the wild garlic and the old fence

Announced our boundary, my dog had halted,
Its skin bristling as it whimpered at nothing,
I should hardly have been very much surprised.
    Who goes there? Only the chalk-faced old man
        Who traps the birds under the fruit-nets

And carries them off inside his stovepipe hat.
And here in dreams comes the doll, Attic Margot,
Who drowned in the watergarden during Lent.
    She's kept her stuffing well over the years
        But the china face has quite collapsed.

'Stop talking about money. You've upset the child.'
But it wasn't that that made me cry. 'Only
A German song we have been learning at school,
   A song about the rooks building their nests
      In the high trees.' The garden is dark

But still the evil crimson of the roses
Shines through. 'I wasn't listening. Suppose
We do suddenly have to leave this old house –
   Why should that worry you? I hate it all,
      And all the children here hate me too.'

I used to think that just by counting windows
And finding secret rooms, I would come across
A clue. One evening I waited in the park
   Expecting a figure with an oil lamp
      To come to the casement and signal.

Now I stroll further afield, beyond the lodge,
And wonder why the villages are empty
And how my father lost all his money.
   I keep meeting a demented beggar
      Who mutters about mouldiwarps

With tears in his eyes. The house is all packed up
Except for one mirror which could not be moved.
In its reflection the brilliant lawns stretch down.
   'Where's that wretched boy?' I'm going now
      And soon I am going to find out.

A Staffordshire Murderer

Every fear is a desire. Every desire is fear.
The cigarettes are burning under the trees
Where the Staffordshire murderers wait for their accomplices
And victims. Every victim is an accomplice.

It takes a lifetime to stroll to the carpark
Stopping at the footbridge for reassurance,
Looking down at the stream observing
(With one eye) the mallard's diagonal progress backwards.

You could cut and run, now. It is not too late.
But your fear is like a long-case clock
In the last whirring second before the hour,
The hammer drawn back, the heart ready to chime.

Fear turns the ignition. The van is unlocked.
You may learn now what you ought to know:
That every journey begins with a death,
That the suicide travels alone, that the murderer needs company.

And the Staffordshire murderers, nervous though they are,
Are masters of the conciliatory smile.
A cigarette? A tablet in a tin?
Would you care for a boiled sweet from the famous poisoner

Of Rugely? These are his own brand.
He has never had any complaints.
He speaks of his victims as a sexual braggart
With a tradesman's emphasis on the word 'satisfaction'.

You are flattered as never before. He appreciates
So much, the little things – your willingness for instance
To bequeath your body at once to his experiments.
He sees the point of you as no one else does.

Large parts of Staffordshire have been undermined.
The trees are in it up to their necks. Fish
Nest in their branches. In one of the Five Towns
An ornamental pond disappeared overnight

Dragging the ducks down with it, down to the old seams
With a sound as of a gigantic bath running out,
Which is in turn the sound of ducks in distress.
Thus History murders mallards, while we hear nothing

Or what we hear we do not understand.
It is heard as the tramp's rage in the crowded precinct:
'Woe to the bloody city of Lichfield.'
It is lost in the enthusiasm of the windows

From which we are offered on the easiest terms
Five times over in colour and once in monochrome

The first reprisals after the drill-sergeant's coup.
How speedily the murder detail makes its way

Along the green beach, past the pink breakers,
And binds the whole cabinet to the oil-drums,
Where death is a preoccupied tossing of the head,
Where no decorative cloud lingers at the gun's mouth.

At the Dame's School dust gathers on the highwayman,
On Sankey and Moody, Wesley and Fox,
On the snoring churchwarden, on Palmer the Poisoner
And Palmer's house and Stanfield Hall.

The brilliant moss has been chipped from the Red Barn.
They say that Cromwell played ping-pong with the cathedral.
We train roses over the arches. In the Minster Pool
Crayfish live under carved stones. Every spring

The rats pick off the young mallards and
The good weather brings out the murderers
By the Floral Clock, by the footbridge,
The pottery murderers in jackets of prussian blue.

'Alack, George, where are thy shoes?'
He lifted up his head and espied the three
Steeple-house spires, and they struck at his life.
And he went by his eye over hedge and ditch

And no one laid hands on him, and he went
Thus crying through the streets, where there seemed
To be a channel of blood running through the streets,
And the market-place appeared like a pool of blood.

For this field of corpses was Lichfield
Where a thousand Christian Britons fell
In Diocletian's day, and and 'much could I write
Of the sense that I had of the blood –'

That winter Friday. Today it is hot.
The cowparsley is so high that the van cannot be seen
From the road. The bubbles rise in the warm canal.
Below the lock-gates you can hear mallards.

A coot hurries along the tow-path, like a Queen's Messenger.
On the heli-pad, an arrival in blue livery
Sends the water-boatmen off on urgent business.
News of a defeat. Keep calm. The cathedral chimes.

The house by the bridge is the house in your dream.
It stares through new frames, unwonted spectacles,
And the paint, you can tell, has been weeping.
In the yard, five striped oildrums. Flowers in a tyre.

This is where the murderer works. But it is Sunday.
Tomorrow's bank holiday will allow the bricks to set.
You see? he has thought of everything. He shows you
The snug little cavity he calls 'your future home'

And 'Do you know,' he remarks, 'I have been counting my
            victims.
Nine hundred and ninety nine, the Number of the Beast!
That makes you . . .' But he sees he has overstepped the mark:
'I'm sorry, but you cannot seriously have thought you were the
            first?'

A thousand preachers, a thousand poisoners,
A thousand martyrs, a thousand murderers –
Surely these preachers are poisoners, these martyrs murderers?
Surely this is all a gigantic mistake?

But there has been no mistake. God and the weather are glorious.
You have come as an anchorite to kneel at your funeral.
Kneel then and pray. The blade flashes a smile.
This is your new life. This murder is yours.

TOM PAULIN

Settlers

They cross from Glasgow to a black city
    Of gantries, mills and steeples. They begin to belong.
He manages the Iceworks, is an elder of the Kirk;
    She becomes, briefly, a cook in Carson's Army.
Some mornings, walking through the company gate,
    He touches the bonnet of a brown lorry.
It is warm. The men watch and say nothing.
    'Queer, how it runs off in the night,'
He says to McCullough, then climbs to his office.
    He stores a warm knowledge on his palm.

    Nightlandings on the Antrim coast, the movement of guns
Now snug in their oiled paper below the floors
    Of sundry kirks and tabernacles in that county.

Under the Eyes

Its retributions work like clockwork
Along murdering miles of terrace-houses
Where someone is saying, 'I am angry,
I am frightened, I am justified.
Every favour, I must repay with interest,
Any slight against myself, the least slip,
Must be balanced out by an exact revenge.'

The city is built on mud and wrath.
Its weather is predicted; its streetlamps
Light up in the glowering, crowded evenings.
Time-switches, ripped from them, are clamped
To sticks of sweet, sweating explosive.
All the machinery of a state
Is a set of scales that squeezes out blood.

Memory is just, too. A complete system
Nothing can surprise. The dead are recalled
From schoolroom afternoons, the hill quarries

Echoing blasts over the secured city;
Or, in a private house, a Judge
Shot in his hallway before his daughter
By a boy who shut his eyes as his hand tightened.

A rain of turds; a pair of eyes; the sky and tears.

Provincial Narratives

The girl's too singular, too passionate,
For him to understand. How can she ever cross that field –
Its warm hays, a sour coolness they bring in cans –
And face him, be with him, when the man's trapped
In a facile childhood, his province of self-love?

So, in the big house, the lady of the arum lilies says,
'Come, I'll be mother. Your father is a sternness
Your mother left. Sit here with me. Kiss me,'
She orders gently. 'I will be good to you.
I will pay you to get away and then come back to me.'

He kneels at her feet. The white hands stroke his hair.
'I blame that bitch my mother. I blame
The paternal mountains and the black earth.
Some abominable collusion got me,
A bedroom huddle that was brief and vicious.'

'Don't say that. You musn't say so,' she lies.
The lilies gape. Such fear! And softness.
A mile outside her lodge-gates, old gruffer
Goes to bed alone. His love has curdled.
His son wants the girl's ambitious coldness,

And her white aunt. She is the moon he follows –
A tyranny of cheekbones, oval eyes
That turn unkind and fix on the hazing lough.
Make me older, he prays. Let me see myself
In my own mirror. Make me more perfect than she is.

In a Northern Landscape

Ingela is thin and she never smiles,
The man is tall and wears the same subdued colours.
Their accents might be anywhere, both seem perfect
And spend only the winter months here.
They own a stone cottage at the end of a field
That slopes to rocks and a gunmetal sea.

Their silence is part of the silence at this season,
Is so wide that these solitaries seem hemmed in
By a distance of empty sea, a bleak mewing
Of gulls perched on their chimney, expecting storm.
They sit in basket chairs on their verandah,
Reading and hearing music from a tiny transistor.

Their isolation is almost visible:
Blue light on snow or sour milk in a cheese-cloth
Resembles their mysterious element.
They pickle herrings he catches, eat sauerkraut
And make love on cold concrete in the afternoons;
Eaters of yoghurt, they enjoy austere pleasures.

At night oil lamps burn in their small windows
And blocks of pressed peat glow in a simple fireplace.
Arc lamps on the new refinery at the point
Answer their lights; there is blackness and the sound of surf.
They are so alike that they have no need to speak,
Like oppressed orphans who have won a fierce privacy.

Dawros Parish Church

They stood at the gate before the service started
And talked together in their Glenties suits,
Smiled shyly at the visitors who packed the church
In summer. A passing congregation
Who mostly knew each other, were sometimes fashionable,
Their sons at prep school, the daughters boarding.
Inside it was as neat and tight as a boat.
Stone flags and whitewashed walls, a little brass.
Old Mrs Flewitt played the organ and Mr Alwell
Read the lessons in an accent as sharp as salt.

O Absalom, Absalom, my son,
An hour is too long, there are too many people,
Too many heads and eyes and thoughts that clutter.

Only one moment counted with the lessons
And that was when, the pressure just too much,
You walked slowly out of that packed church
Into bright cold air.
Then, before the recognitions and the talk,
There was an enormous sight of the sea,
A silent water beyond society.

Trotsky in Finland
(an incident from his memoirs)

The pension is very quiet. It is called
Rauha, meaning 'peace' in Finnish.
The air is transparent, perfecting
The pine trees and lakes.
He finds himself admiring the stillness
Of a pure landscape. He consumes it.
A bourgeois moment. It might be somewhere Swiss,
The wooden cuckoos calling to an uneventful
Absence, their polyglot puns
Melting in Trieste or Zürich.

The last days of autumn. The Swedish writer
Adds another sonnet to his cycle.
His English mistress drifts through the garden.
An actress, she admires her face
Bloomed in the smooth lake.
At night her giggles and frills dismay
The strictness of minor art.

They leave without paying their bill.

The owner chases them to Helsingfors.
His invisible wife is lying in the room
Above – they must give her champagne
To keep her heart beating, but she dies
While her husband screams for his money.

The head-waiter sets out to find him.
Leaving a crate of gilded bottles
By the corpse upstairs.
                The silence here.
A thick snow is falling, the house
Is a dead monument. Insanely traditional.

He is completely alone. At nightfall
The postman carries a storm in his satchel:
St Petersburg papers – the strike is spreading.
He asks the thin boy for his bill.
He calls for horses. Thinking,
'If this were a fiction, it would be Byron
Riding out of the Tivoli Gardens, his rank
And name set aside. Forced by more than himself.'

He crosses the frontier and speaks
To a massed force at the Institute,

Plunging from stillness into history.

Anastasia McLaughlin

Her father is sick. He dozes most afternoons.
The nurse makes tea then and scans *The Newsletter*.
She has little to say to his grey daughter
Whose name began a strangeness the years took over.
His trade was flax and yarns, he brought her name
With an ikon and *matrioshka* – gifts for his wife
Who died the year that Carson's statue was unveiled.

McLaughlin is dreaming of a sermon he once heard
From a righteous preacher in a wooden pulpit
Who frowned upon a sinful brotherhood and shouted
The Word of deserts and rainy places where the Just
Are stretched to do the work a hard God sent them for.
His text was taken from the land of Uz
Where men are upright and their farms are walled.

'Though we may make sand to melt in a furnace
And make a mirror of it, we are as shadows
Thrown by a weaver's shuttle: and though we hide ourselves
In desolate cities and in empty houses,

His anger will seek us out till we shall hear
The accent of the destroyer, the sly champing
Of moths busy with the linen in our chests.'

He wakes to a dull afternoon like any other –
The musty dampness of his study, the window panes
That flaw his view of the lawn and settled trees.
The logs in the grate have turned to a soft ash.
The dour gardener who cut them is smoking
In the warm greenhouse, wondering did his nephew
Sleak in the week before and thieve McLaughlin's silver?

Constables came to the Mill House with alsatians,
And the wet spring was filled with uniforms and statements.
When they found nothing, they suspected everyone.
Even the plain woman who served them tea.
'Father, I am the lost daughter whose name you stole.
Your visions slide across these walls: dry lavender,
Flaked memories of all that wronged us. I am unkind.'

He sees his son below the bruised Atlantic,
And on a summer's morning in Great Victoria Street
He talks with Thomas Ferguson outside the Iceworks.
He sees the north stretched out upon the mountains,
Its dream of fair weather rubbing a bloom on rinsed slates;
He watches the mills prosper and grow derelict,
As he starts his journey to the Finland Station.

The Harbour in the Evening

The bereaved years, they've settled to this
Bay-windowed guest house by the harbour wall.
Each of us loved a man who died,
Then learnt how to be old and seem cheerful.
I think of being young, in the coastguard station.
Those cement cottages with the washing
Swaying in the sea wind. What can she see,
The girl I talk to? Victorian childhoods
Where little stick figures go flickering
Along the roads? Such eagerness that used to be.
A butcher's shop, a boarding house, the dead
Are smiling from the windows there.

So many names, faces, and used things.
Dry calico, the smell of cedar wood . . .
I keep them in a drowsy kind of wisdom.
I have my drawer of rings and photographs.

The waves rustle on the beach like starched silk.
And girls come walking down a staircase
Into a wide room where lamps are burning.
Love was a danger and then children.
At sunset, when I saw the white beacon
On the quay, I felt a tear starting.
But I was happy like a woman who opens a door
And hears music. It was your face I saw.
I heard your voice, its gentleness.
And I stared over the water at another coast,
An old woman in a sleep of voices.

Atlantic Changelings

The breakers, the marram dunes,
A sea snipe beating over green water,
Footprints of passing visitors
On a curved strand . . . I trace them now
Like a hunched detective scowling
In a dead resort, and learn the gossip
Of a social summer – see this walled pit
Scooped by that peculiar child
No one invited to their sandy picnic.
See where Long walked his dog last evening
And where the professor's wife met him
By the tideline. They exchanged polite words
On its drift of dry shells, though a sea potato
In the likeness of a shaved pudendum
Splintered their good manners.

Far from their different societies
The scuffed patterns of these prints
Show everyone changed into transparent
Shadows, meeting on this shore.
Their inquisitive uplifted faces
Challenge and beckon with a shy

Confidence, their soothed voices
Come floating from the class
I could belong to (like them I have left
The city to consume a wild landscape).
We will pack soon and the sly locals
Will repossess this expensive view.
In the windy now I hug my righteousness
Like a thermos flask. I cry out
For a great change in nature.

Second-Rate Republics

The dull ripe smell of gas,
A pile of envelopes fading
On the hall table – no one
In this rented atmosphere remembers
The names who once gave this address.

We might be forgotten already,
She thinks, as she climbs the stairs
To spend a long weekend with him.
The trees in these brick avenues
Are showing full and green
Against the windows of partitioned rooms.
The air is humid, and down the street
She hears the single bark
Of a car door slamming shut.

He touches her and she sees herself
Being forced back into a shabby city
Somewhere else in Europe: how clammy
It is, how the crowds press and slacken
On the pavement, shaking photographs
Of a statesman's curdled face.

Now there is only a thin sheet
Between their struggling bodies
And the stained mattress.
Now his face hardens like a photograph,
And in the distance she hears
The forced jubilance of a crowd
That is desolate and obedient.

A Lyric Afterwards

There was a taut dryness all that summer
and you sat each day in the hot garden
until those uniformed comedians
filled the street with their big white ambulance,
fetching you and bringing you back to me.

Far from the sea of ourselves we waited
and prayed for the tight blue silence to give.
In your absence I climbed to a square room
where there were dried flowers, folders of sonnets
and crossword puzzles: call them musical

snuffboxes or mannered anachronisms,
they were all too uselessly intricate,
caskets of the dead spirit. Their bitter
constraints and formal pleasures were a style
of being perfect in despair; they spoke

with the vicious trapped crying of a wren.
But that is changed now, and when I see you
walking by the river, a step from me,
there is this great kindness everywhere:
now in the grace of the world and always.

JEFFREY WAINWRIGHT

1815

I. The Mill-Girl

Above her face
Dead roach stare vertically
Out of the canal.
Water fills her ears,
Her nose her open mouth.
Surfacing, her bloodless fingers
Nudge the drying gills.

The graves have not
A foot's width between them.
Apprentices, jiggers, spinners
Fill them straight from work,
Common as smoke.

Waterloo is all the rage;
Coal and iron and wool
Have supplied the English miracle.

II. Another Part of the Field

The dead on all sides –
The fallen –
The deep-chested rosy ploughboys
Swell out of their uniforms.

The apple trees,
That were dressed overall,
Lie stripped about their heads.

'The French cavalry
Came up very well my lord.'
'Yes. And they went down
Very well too.
Overturned like turtles.
Our muskets were obliged
To their white bellies.'

No flies on Wellington.
His spruce wit sits straight
In the saddle, jogging by.

III. The Important Man

Bothered by his wife
From a good dinner,
The lock-keeper goes down
To his ponderous water's edge
To steer in the new corpse.

A bargee, shouting to be let through,
Stumps over the bulging lengths
Of his hatches,
Cursing the slowness
Of water.

The lock-keeper bends and pulls her out
With his bare hands.
Her white eyes, rolled upwards,
Just stare.

He is an important man now.
He turns to his charge:
The water flows uphill.

IV. Death of the Mill-Owner

Shaking the black earth
From a root of potatoes,
The gardener walks
To the kitchen door.

The trees rattle
Their empty branches together.

Upstairs the old man
Is surprised.
His fat body clenches –
Mortified
At what is happening.

Thomas Müntzer
for David Spooner

Thomas Müntzer was a Protestant reformer in the early years of the German Reformation. He was a radical and a visionary both in theology and politics for whom religious thought and experience became integrated with ideas and movements towards social revolution.

Travelling through Germany, preaching and writing, continually in trouble with the authorities, he came to support and lead struggles by common people against the monopolies of wealth and learning. In 1525, in the Peasant War, he led an army against the princes which was heavily defeated at Frankenhausen. Müntzer was subsequently captured and executed.

Doubt is the Water, the movement to good and evil. Who swims on the water without a saviour is between life and death

(MÜNTZER)

I have seen in my solitude very clear things that are not true.

(MACHADO)

I

Just above where my house sits on the slope
Is a pond, a lodge when the mine was here,
Now motionless, secretive, hung in weeds.

Sometimes on clear nights I spread my arms wide
And can fly, stiff but perfect, down
Over this pond just an inch above the surface.

When I land I have just one, two drops of water
On my beard. I am surprised how quick
I have become a flier, a walker on air.

II

I see my brother crawling in the woods
To gather snails' shells. *This is not
A vision.* Look carefully and you can tell

How he is caught in the roots of a tree
Whose long branches spread upwards bearing as
Fruit gardeners and journeymen, merchants

And lawyers, jewellers and bishops,
Cardinals chamberlains nobles princes
Branch by branch kings pope and emperor.

III

I feel the very earth is against me.
Night after night she turns in my sleep
And litters my fields with stones.

I lie out all summer spread like a coat
Over the earth one night after another
Waiting to catch her. And then

She is mine and the rowan blooms –
His black roots swim out and dive to subdue her –
His red blood cracks in the air and saves me.

IV

How many days did I search in my books
For such power, crouched like a bird under
My roof and lost to the world?

Scholars say God no longer speaks with us
Men – as though he has grown dumb, lost his tongue,
(Cut out for stealing a hare or a fish?)

Now I explode – out of this narrow house,
My mind lips hands skin my whole body
Cursing them for their flesh and their learning –

V

dran dran dran we have the sword – the purity
Of metal – the beauty of blood falling.
Spilt it is refreshed, it freshens also

The soil which when we turn it will become
Paradise for us once rid of these maggots
And their blind issue. They will seek about

And beg you: 'Why is this happening to us?
Forgive us Forgive us', pleading now for
Mercy a new sweet thing they've found a taste for.

VI

So you see from this how I am – Müntzer:
'O bloodthirsty man' breathing not air
But fire and slaughter, a true phantasist –

'A man born for heresy and schism',
'This most lying of men', 'a mad dog'.
And all because I speak and say: God made

All men free with His own blood shed.
Hold everything in common. Share evil.
And I find I am a god, like all men.

VII

He teaches the gardener from his trees
And the fisherman from his catch, even
The goldsmith from the testing of his gold.

In the pond the cold thick water clothes me.
I live with the timorous snipe, beetles
And skaters, the pike smiles and moves with me.

We hold it in common without jealousy.
Touch your own work and the simple world.
In these unread creatures sings the real gospel.

VIII

I have two guilders for a whole winter.
I ask for company and food from beggars,
The very poorest, those I fancy most

Blessed . . . I am in love with a girl
And dare not tell her so . . . she makes me
Like a boy again – sick and dry-mouthed.

How often have I told you God comes only
In your apparent abandonment. This is
The misery of my exile – I was elected to it.

IX

My son will not sleep. The noise
And every moving part of the world
Shuttles round him, making him regard it,

Giving him – only four years old! – no peace.
He moves quietly in his own purposes
Yet stays joyless. There is no joy to be had,

And he knows that and is resigned to it.
At his baptism we dressed him in white
And gave him salt as a symbol of this wisdom.

X

I am white and broken. I can hardly gasp out
What I want to say, which is: *I believe in God* . . .
At Frankenhausen His promised rainbow

Did bloom in the sky, silky and so bold
No one could mistake it. Seeing it there
I thought I could catch their bullets in my hands.

An article of faith. I was found in bed
And carried here for friendly
Interrogation. They ask me *what I believe.*

XI

Their horsemen ride over our crops kicking
The roots from the ground. They poison wells
And throw fire down the holes where people hide.

An old woman crawls out. She is bleeding
And screaming so now they say they are sorry
And would like to bandage her. She won't

Go with them. She struggles free. *I see it
I see it* – she is bound to die . . .
This is the glittering night we wake in.

XII

I lie here for a few hours yet, clothed still
In my external life, flesh I have tried
To render pure, and a scaffold of bones.

I would resign all interest in it.
To have any love for my own fingered
Body and brain is a luxury.

History, which is Eternal Life, is what
We need to celebrate. Stately tearful
Progress . . . you've seen how I have wept for it.

A Hymn to Liberty

Count all the miner's hours, all his breathing
To the point of light.

A scud of air across the water's open face;
A child dabbles the flats of her palms
And laughs as she watches their play.
Each tree its silence breaks.

The movement of a breath of air across the lips
Creates the mind, and gives all of us our lives –

The inspired Republic,
A commune like the body with the air.

The child in love with the endless lake
Draws all her breath

ANDREW MOTION

In the Attic

Even though we know now
your clothes will never
be needed, we keep them,
upstairs in a locked trunk.

Sometimes I kneel there,
holding them, trying to relive
time you wore them, to remember
the actual shape of arm and wrist.

My hands push down between
hollow, invisible sleeves,
hesitate, then lift
patterns of memory:

a green holiday, a red christening,
all your unfinished lives
fading through dark summers,
entering my head as dust.

The Legacy

Ashes have scattered her,
her money disowns her,
but I sit down to write
at the desk she willed me,
watching the lamp resurrect
her glistening lives:

layer after layer I inherit
their light immortality,
where in the end my hand
will sign my furniture on
to children or friends,
before it stops still as hers,

and then is replaced again
in distant, unvisited rooms,

transcribing itself for ever
like shadows which follow it now,
uncurling themselves in silence
on printed paper and skin.

One Life

Up country, her husband is working late
on a high cool veranda. His radio plays
World Service News, but he does not listen,
and does not notice how moonlight fills
the plain below, with its ridge of trees
and shallow river twisting to Lagos
a whole night's journey south. What holds
him instead are these prizes that patience
and stealthy love have caught: *papilio
dardanus* – each with the blacks and whites
of simple absolutes he cannot match.

She understands nothing of this.
Away in her distant room, she lies
too sick to see the bar-sign steadily print
its purple letters over and over her wall,
too tired to care when the silence breaks
and this stranger, her friend, leans smiling
above the bed. There is just one implausible
thought that haunts her as clear and perfect
as ever – the delicate pottery bowl she left
forgotten at home, still loaded with apples
and pears she knows by their English names.

Anne Frank Huis

Even now, after twice her lifetime of grief
and anger in the very place, whoever comes
to climb these narrow stairs, discovers how
the bookcase slides aside, then walks through
shadow into sunlit rooms, can never help

but break her secrecy again. Just listening
is a kind of guilt. The Westerkerk repeats
itself outside, as if all time worked round
towards her fear, and made each stroke die
down on guarded streets. Imagine it –

three years of whispering and loneliness
and plotting, day by day, the Allied line
in Europe with a yellow chalk. What hope
she had for ordinary love and interest
survives her here, displayed above the bed

as pictures of her family; some actors;
fashions chosen by Princess Elizabeth.
And those who stoop to see them find
not only patience missing its reward,
but one enduring wish for chances like

my own: to leave as simply as I do,
and walk where couples drift at ease
up dusty tree-lined avenues, or watch
a silent barge come clear of bridges
settling their reflections in the blue canal.

Bathing at Glymenopoulo

Lotophagi. I can believe it:
first moment ashore the heat
stunned us – a lavish blast
and the stink of horses.
Then it was *Mister. Mister.
Captain McKenzie* – bathing girls
round from the beach, white
towels and parasols weaving
through gun-carriages, crates
and saddlery lined on the quay
to pelt us with flowers. *Want
Captain McKenzie? I give you
good times*. But we rode away,
eyes-front and smiling, pursued
until the Majestic gates.

Men to the grounds, officers
one to a cool high-ceilinged room –
mine with a balcony looking
down to the lake. There were pelicans
clambering carefully in and out
and in, never still, wrecking
the stagnant calm, fighting,
and shaking their throats
with a flabby rattle. Otherwise,
peace – the cedar layered
in enormous green-black slabs
and shading tents on the lawn;
the horses only a rumour –
stamping and snorting
out by the kitchen garden.

Each morning we rode early
to Christmas Hill – two hours
of dressage in dusty circuits
then home with the sun still low.
For the rest, time was our own –
no orders, no news from France,
but delicious boredom: polo
some evenings, and long afternoons
bathing at Glymenopoulo. Iras,
I have you by heart, giggling
and stumbling up from the breakers
into my photograph, one thin hand
pressed to your cheek, your knee-
length, navy-blue costume puckered
and clinging. I singled you out

day after day after day –
to swim with, to dawdle
arm in arm on the beach
as the furious sun sank, and later
to hear your pidgin whispers
dancing in waterfront cafés:
You not like anyone. Gentling
than other Captain McKenzies.
You not like others –

your lemon-smelling hair
loose and brushing my mouth,
your bracelets clinking,
and langorous slow waltzes
twirling us round and round
in the smoky half-light. *Luck*.

I kept telling myself. *Luck*.
It will end – but the lazy days
stretched into months,
and then we were riding out
on a clear pastel-blue morning
to Christmas Hill as ever.
And half-way, at Kalia,
stopped at our watering place –
a date-grove fringing the pool,
and the whole platoon fanned
in a crescent to drink.
I was dismounted, leading my horse
over packed sand, empty-headed
and waving flies from my face
when the firing began. Ten shots,

perhaps – flips and smacks
into date-trunks or puffing the sand
and nobody hurt. But we charged –
all of us thinking *At last. Action
at last*, as our clumsy light brigade
wheeled under the trees and away
up a steady slope. I was far left,
drawing my sword with a stupid
high-pitched yelp as we laboured
through silvery mirage lakes.
They were waiting ahead –
Senussi, no more than a dozen,
their gypsy silhouettes crouching
and slinking back into stones
as we breasted the rise.

The end of the world. A sheer
wall falling hundreds of feet
to a haze of yellow scrub.
I wrenched myself round, sword

dropped, head low, to a dead
teetering halt as our line
staggered, and buckled, and broke
in a clattering slide. I can
hear it again – the panicking
whinnies, shouts, and the rush
of scree where they shambled off
into space. It has taken three days
to bury them – one for the trek
to the valley floor, one to scratch
their ranks of graves, one to return.

There is little the same. At six
we have curfew now: I am writing this
after dark on my knee in the School
of Instruction grounds, in a tent.
I cannot sleep – sirens disturb me,
groaning up from the harbour.
Those are the ships from Gallipoli,
unloading their trail of stretchers
to the Majestic, where you will be
waiting, Iras, I know, stopped
outside the gates, high-heeled
just as you were, with your hair
fluffed out after swimming, repeating
your tender sluttish call, *Want
Captain McKenzie? I give you good times.*

PAUL MULDOON

Elizabeth

The birds begin as an isolated shower
Over the next county, their slow waltz
Swerving as if to avoid something
Every so often, getting thin
As it slants, making straight for
Us over your father's darkening fields,
Till their barely visible wings
Remember themselves, they are climbing again.
We wonder what could bring them so far

Inland, they belong to the sea.
You hold on hard like holding on to life,
Following the flock as it bends
And collapses like a breeze.
You want to know where from and why,
But birds would never keep still long enough
For me to be able to take a count.
We'll hold our ground and they'll pass.
But they're coming right overhead, you cry,

And storm inside and bang the door.
All I can hear is the flicking of bolts.
The one dull window is shutting
Its eye as if a wayward hurricane
With the name of a girl and the roar
Of devils were beginning its assaults.
But these are the birds of a child's painting,
Filling the page till nothing else is seen.
You are inside yet, pacing the floor,

Having been trapped in every way.
You hold yourself as your own captive.
My promised children are in your hands,
Hostaged by you in your father's old house.
I call you now for all the names of the day,
Lizzie and Liz and plain Beth.

You do not make the slightest sound.
When you decide that you have nothing to lose
And come out, there is nothing you can say,

We watch them hurtle, a recklessness of stars,
Into the acre that has not cooled
From my daylong ploughings and harrowings,
Their greys flecking the brown,
Till one, and then two, and now four
Sway back across your father's patchwork quilt,
Into your favourite elm. They will stay long
Enough to underline how soon they will be gone,
As you seem thinner than you were before.

Identities

When I reached the sea
I fell in with another who had just come
From the interior. Her family
Had figured in a past regime
But her father was now imprisoned.

She had travelled, only by night,
Escaping just as her own warrant
Arrived and stealing the police boat,
As far as this determined coast.

As it happened, we were staying at the same
Hotel, pink and goodish for the tourist
Quarter. She came that evening to my room
Asking me to go to the capital,
Offering me wristwatch and wallet,
To search out an old friend who would steal
Papers for herself and me. Then to be married,
We could leave from that very harbour.

I have been wandering since, back up the streams
That had once flowed simply one into the other,
One taking the other's name.

Mules

Should they not have the best of both worlds?

Her feet of clay gave the lie
To the star burned in our mare's brow.
Would Parsons' jackass not rest more assured
That cross wrenched from his shoulders?

We had loosed them into one field.
I watched Sam Parsons and my quick father
Tense for the punch below their belts,
For what was neither one thing or the other.

It was as though they had shuddered
To think of their gaunt, sexless foal
Dropped tonight in the cowshed.

We might yet claim that it sprang from earth
Were it not for the afterbirth
Trailed like some fine, silk parachute,
That we would know from what heights it fell.

Paris

A table for two will scarcely seat
The pair of us! All the people we have been
Are here as guests, strategically deployed
As to who will go best with whom.
A convent girl, a crashing bore, the couple

Who aren't quite all they seem.
A last shrimp curls and winces on your plate
Like an embryo. 'Is that a little overdone?'
And these country faces at the window
That were once our own. They study the menu,

Smile faintly, and are gone.
Chicken Marengo! It's a far cry from the Moy.

'There's no such person as Saint Christopher,
Father Talbot gave it out at Mass.
Same as there's no such place as Limbo.'

The world's less simple for being travelled,
Though. In each fresh, neutral place
Where our differences might have been settled
There were men sitting down to talk of peace
Who began with the shape of the table.

The Big House

I was only the girl under the stairs
But I was the first to notice something was wrong.
I was always first up and about, of course.
Those hens would never lay two days running
In the same place. I would rise early
And try round the haggard for fresh nests.
The mistress let me keep the egg-money.

And that particular night there were guests,
Mrs de Groot from the bridge set
And a young man who wrote stories for children,
So I wanted everything to be just right
When they trooped down to breakfast that morning.

I slept at the very top of that rambling house,
A tiny room with only a sky-light window.
I had brushed my hair and straightened my dress
And was just stepping into the corridor
When it struck me. That old boarded-up door
Was flung open. A pile of rubble and half-bricks
Was strewn across the landing floor.

I went on down. I was stooping among the hay-stacks
When there came a clatter of hooves in the yard.
The squire's sure-footed little piebald mare
Had found her own way home, as always.
He swayed some. Then fell headlong on the cobbles.

There was not so much as the smell of whiskey on him.
People still hold he had died of fright,
That the house was haunted by an elder brother
Who was murdered for his birthright.
People will always put two and two together.

What I remember most of that particular morning
Was how calmly everyone took the thing.
The mistress insisted that life would go on quietly
As it always had done. Breakfast was served
At nine exactly. I can still hear Mrs de Groot
Telling how she had once bid seven hearts.
The young man's stories were for grown-ups, really.

Palm Sunday

To tell the range of the English longbows
At Agincourt, or Crécy,
We need look no further than the yews
That, even in Irish graveyards,
Are bent on Fitzwilliams, and de Courcys.
These are the date-palms of the North.

They grow where nothing really should.
No matter how many are gathered
They never make a wood.
The coffin-board that yearns to be a tree
Goes on to bear no small, sweet gourds
As might be trampled by another Christ.

Today's the day for all such entrances.
I was wondering if you'd bring me through
To a world where everything stands
For itself, and carries
Just as much weight as me on you.
My scrawny door-mat. My deep, red carpet.

Why Brownlee Left

Why Brownlee left, and where he went,
Is a mystery even now.
For if a man should have been content
It was him; two acres of barley,
One of potatoes, four bullocks,
A milker, a slated farmhouse.
He was last seen going out to plough
On a March morning, bright and early.

By noon Brownlee was famous;
They had found all abandoned, with
The last rig unbroken, his pair of black
Horses, like man and wife,
Shifting their weight from foot to
Foot, and gazing into the future.

Cuba

My eldest sister arrived home that morning
In her white muslin evening dress.
'Who the hell do you think you are,
Running out to dances in next to nothing?
As though we hadn't enough bother
With the world at war, if not at an end.'
My father was pounding the breakfast-table.

'Those Yankees were touch and go as it was –
If you'd heard Patton in Armagh –
But this Kennedy's nearly an Irishman
So he's not much better than ourselves.
And him with only to say the word.
If you've got anything on your mind
Maybe you should make your peace with God.'

I could hear May from beyond the curtain.
'Bless me, Father, for I have sinned.

I told a lie once, I was disobedient once.
And, Father, a boy touched me once.'
'Tell me, child. Was this touch immodest?
Did he touch your breast, for example?'
'He brushed against me, Father. Very gently.'

Quoof

How often have I carried our family word
For the hot water bottle
To a strange bed,
As my father would juggle a red-hot half-brick
In an old sock
To his childhood settle.
I have taken it into so many lovely heads
Or laid it between us like a sword.

A hotel room in New York City
With a girl who spoke hardly any English,
My hand on her breast
Like the smouldering one-off spoor of the yeti
Or some other shy beast
That has yet to enter the language.

Immram

I was fairly and squarely behind the eight
That morning in Foster's pool-hall
When it came to me out of the blue
In the shape of a sixteen-ounce billiard cue
That lent what he said some little weight.
'Your old man was an ass-hole.
That makes an ass-hole out of you.'
My grand-father hailed from New York State.
My grand-mother was part Cree.
This must be some new strain in my pedigree.

The billiard-player had been big, and black,
Dressed to kill, or inflict a wound,
And had hung around the pin-table
As long as it took to smoke a panatella.
I was clinging to an ice-pack
On which the Titanic might have floundered
When I was suddenly bedazzled
By a little silver knick-knack
That must have fallen from his hat-band.
I am telling this exactly as it happened.

I suppose that I should have called the cops
Or called it a day and gone home
And done myself, and you, a favour.
But I wanted to know more about my father.
So I drove west to Paradise
Where I was greeted by the distant hum
Of *Shall We Gather at the River?*
The perfect introduction to the kind of place
Where people go to end their lives.
It might have been *Bringing In the Sheaves.*

My mother had just been fed by force,
A pint of lukewarm water through a rubber hose.
I hadn't seen her in six months or a year,
Not since my father had disappeared.
Now she'd taken an overdose
Of alcohol and barbiturates,
And this, I learned, was her third.
I was told then by a male nurse
That if I came back at the end of the week
She might be able to bring herself to speak.

Which brought me round to the Atlantic Club.
The Atlantic Club was an old grain-silo
That gave onto the wharf.
Not the kind of place you took your wife
Unless she had it in mind to strip
Or you had a mind to put her up for sale.
I knew how my father had come here by himself

And maybe thrown a little crap
And watched his check double, and treble,
With highball hard on the heels of highball.

She was wearing what looked like a dead fox
Over a low-cut sequinned gown,
And went by the name of Susan, or Suzanne.
A girl who would never pass out of fashion
So long as there's an 'if' in California.
I stood her one or two pink gins
And the talk might have come round to passion
Had it not been for a pair of thugs
Who suggested that we both take a wander,
She upstairs, I into the wild, blue yonder.

They came bearing down on me out of nowhere.
A Buick and a Chevrolet.
They were heading towards a grand slam.
Salami on rye. I was the salami.
So much for my faith in human nature.
The age of chivalry how are you?
But I side-stepped them, neatly as Salome,
So they came up against one another
In a moment of intense heat and light,
Like a couple of turtles on their wedding-night.

Both were dead. Of that I was almost certain.
When I looked into their eyes
I sensed the import of their recent visions,
How you must get all of wisdom
As you pass through a wind-shield.
One's frizzled hair was dyed
A peroxide blond, his sinewy arms emblazoned
With tattoos, his vest marked *Urgent*.
All this was taking on a shape
That might be clearer after a night's sleep.

When the only thing I had ever held in common
With anyone else in the world
Was the ramshackle house on Central Boulevard
That I shared with my child-bride

Until she dropped out to join a commune,
You can imagine how little I was troubled
To kiss Goodbye to its weathered clap-board.
When I nudged the rocker on the porch
It rocked as though it might never rest.
It seemed that I would forever be driving west.

I was in luck. She'd woken from her slumbers
And was sitting out among flowering shrubs.
All might have been peace and harmony
In that land of milk and honey
But for the fact that our days are numbered,
But for Foster's, the Atlantic Club,
And now, that my father owed Redpath money.
Redpath. She told me how his empire
Ran a little more than half-way to Hell
But began on the top floor of the Park Hotel.

Steel and glass were held in creative tension
That afternoon in the Park.
I strode through the cavernous lobby
And found myself behind a nervous couple
Who registered as Mr and Mrs Alfred Tennyson.
The unsmiling, balding desk-clerk
Looked like a man who would sell an alibi
To King Kong on the Empire State building,
So I thought better of passing the time of day.
I took the elevator all the way.

You remember how, in a half-remembered dream,
You found yourself in a long corridor,
How behind the first door there was nothing,
Nothing behind the second,
Then how you swayed from room to empty room
Until, beyond that last half-open door
You heard a telephone . . . and you were wakened
By a woman's voice asking you to come
To the Atlantic Club, between six and seven,
And when you came, to come alone.

I was met, not by the face behind the voice,
But by yet another aide-de-camp
Who would have passed for a Barbary pirate
With a line in small-talk like a parrot
And who ferried me past an outer office
To a not ungracious inner sanctum.
I did a breast-stroke through the carpet,
Went under once, only to surface
Alongside the raft of a banquet-table –
A whole roast pig, its mouth fixed on an apple.

Beyond the wall-length, two-way mirror
There was still more to feast your eyes upon
As Susan, or Susannah, danced
Before what looked like an invited audience,
A select band of admirers
To whom she would lay herself open.
I was staring into the middle distance
Where two men and a dog were mowing her meadow
When I was hit by a hypodermic syringe.
And I entered a world equally rich and strange.

There was one who can only have been asleep
Among row upon row of sheeted cadavers
In what might have been the Morgue
Of all the cities of America,
Who beckoned me towards her slab
And silently drew back the covers
On the vermilion omega
Where she had been repeatedly stabbed,
Whom I would carry over the threshold of pain
That she might come and come and come again.

I came to, under a steaming pile of trash
In the narrow alley-way
Behind that old Deep Water Baptist mission
Near the corner of Sixteenth and Ocean –
A blue-eyed boy, the Word made flesh
Amid no hosannahs nor hallelujahs
But the strains of Blind Lemon Jefferson

That leaked from the church
Through a hole in a tiny, stained-glass window,
In what was now a torrent, now had dwindled.

And honking to Blind Lemon's blues guitar
Was a solitary, black cat
Who would have turned the heads of Harlem.
He was no louder than a fire-alarm,
A full-length coat of alligator,
An ermine stole, his wide-brimmed hat
Festooned with family heirlooms.
I watch him trickle a fine, white powder
Into his palm, so not a grain would spill,
Then snort it through a rolled-up dollar bill.

This was angel dust, dust from an angel's wing
Where it glanced off the land of cocaine,
Be that Bolivia, Peru.
Or snow from the slopes of the Andes, so pure
It would never melt in spring.
But you know how over every Caliban
There's Ariel, and behind him, Prospero;
Everyone taking a cut, dividing and conquering
With lactose and dextrose,
Everyone getting right up everyone else's nose.

I would tip-toe round by the side of the church
For a better view. Some fresh cement.
I trod as lightly there
As a mere mortal at Grauman's Chinese Theatre.
An oxy-acetylene torch.
There were two false-bottomed
Station-waggons. I watched Mr See-You-Later
Unload a dozen polythene packs
From one to the other. *The Urgent Shipping Company.*
It behooved me to talk to the local P.D.

'My father, God rest him, he held this theory
That the Irish, the American Irish,
Were really the thirteenth tribe,
The Israelites of Europe.

All along, my father believed in fairies
But he might as well have been Jewish.'
His laugh was a slight hiccup.
I guessed that Lieutenant Brendan O'Leary's
Grand-mother's pee was green,
And that was why she had to leave old Skibbereen.

Now, what was all this about the Atlantic cabaret,
Urgent, the top floor of the Park?
When had I taken it into my head
That somebody somewhere wanted to see me dead?
Who? No, Redpath was strictly on the level.
So why, rather than drag in the Narcs.,
Why didn't he and I drive over to Ocean Boulevard
At Eighteenth Street, or wherever?
Would I mind stepping outside while he made a call
To such-and-such a luminary at City Hall?

I counted thirty-odd of those brown-eyed girls
Who ought to be in pictures,
Bronzed, bleached, bare-breasted,
Bare-assed to a man,
All sitting, crossed-legged, in a circle
At the feet of this life-guard out of Big Sur
Who made an exhibition
Of his dorsals and his pectorals
While one by one his disciples took up the chant
The Lord is my surf-board. I shall not want.

He went on to explain to O'Leary and myself
How only that morning he had acquired the lease
On the old Baptist mission,
Though his was a wholly new religion.
He called it *The Way of The One Wave*.
This one wave was sky-high, like a wall of glass,
And had come to him in a vision.
You could ride forever, effortlessly.
The Lieutenant was squatting before his new guru.
I would inform the Missing Persons Bureau.

His name? I already told you his name.
Forty-nine. Fifty come July.
Five ten or eleven. One hundred and eighty pounds.
He could be almost anyone.
And only now was it brought home to me
How rarely I looked in his eyes,
Which were hazel. His hair was mahogany brown.
There was a scar on his left forearm
From that time he got himself caught in the works
Of a saw-mill near Ithaca, New York.

I was just about getting things into perspective
When a mile-long white Cadillac
Came sweeping out of the distant past
Like a wayward Bay mist,
A transport of joy. There was that chauffeur
From the 1931 Sears Roebuck catalogue,
Susannah, as you guessed,
And this refugee from F. Scott Fitzgerald
Who looked as if he might indeed own the world.
His name was James Earl Caulfield III.

This was how it was. My father had been a mule.
He had flown down to Rio
Time and time again. But he courted disaster.
He tried to smuggle a wooden statue
Through the airport at Lima.
The Christ of the Andes. The statue was hollow.
He stumbled. It went and shattered.
And he had to stand idly by
As a cool fifty or sixty thousand dollars worth
Was trampled back into the good earth.

He would flee, to La Paz, then to Buenos Aires,
From alias to alias.
I imagined him sitting outside a hacienda
Somewhere in the Argentine.
He would peer for hours
Into the vastness of the pampas.
Or he might be pointing out the constellations

Of the Southern hemisphere
To the open-mouthed child at his elbow.
He sleeps with a loaded pistol under his pillow.

The mile-long white Cadillac had now wrapped
Itself round the Park hotel.
We were spirited to the nineteenth floor
Where Caulfield located a secret door.
We climbed two perilous flights of steps
To the exclusive penthouse suite.
A moment later I was ushered
Into a chamber sealed with black drapes.
As I grew accustomed to the gloom
I realized there was someone else in the room.

He was huddled on an old orthopaedic mattress,
The makings of a skeleton,
Naked but for a pair of draw-string shorts.
His hair was waistlength, as was his beard.
He was covered in bedsores.
He raised one talon.
'I forgive you,' he croaked. 'And I forget.
On your way out, you tell that bastard
To bring me a dish of ice-cream.
I want Baskin-Robbins banana-nut ice-cream.'

I shimmied about the cavernous lobby.
Mr and Mrs Alfred Tennyson
Were ahead of me through the revolving door.
She tipped the bell-hop five dollars.
There was a steady stream of people
That flowed in one direction,
Faster and deeper,
That I would go along with, happily,
As I made my way back, like any other pilgrim,
To Main Street, to Foster's pool-room.

PETER SCUPHAM

Early Summer

Small things get lost now;
There are intrusions,
Defeats in alien worlds.

This is the time to slide a foolish leaf
Under the flimsy legs that ruck
The pond's tight skin,

Or bury the grassed fledgeling,
Tender for the closed eyes, the ungainly head
On the lax grey neck.

The rambling bee, obtuse and hairy,
Unzips with his dull purr
The studious air.

He too will need us.
We hoist him to a window, smile
At his diminuendo horn.

Papery moths drift to the light,
Churr in a hand's cave,
Then out, out.

Later, much later, we shall assault the wasps,
Brewing them in our slow cauldrons
Of honey, vinegar.

The Old Pantry

Sun angles for a perch of glass,
Cups alight on their scroll hooks.

Life transfers to bone china
Her sparkling buds and lustres.

Oilcloth glistens to cut scraps of light,
A dimmed or glittering stillness,

But from the dark, the recessed silence,
White food floats dim surfaces.

Anchored at the pitcher's rim, a ladle
Swings a gleam over sweet milk,

Sugar crumbles a cold silver-sand,
New-baked bread swells under damp cloths.

An underworld, bleached and dumb,
Reaching into this fresh wash of air.

The Secret

The wagtail's semaphore in black and white,
A diadem spider, tense on corded dew,
Globular clusters of slow snails, clambering
At the wall's foot:
The daylight, filled with speaking likenesses.

Yet the dusk found him clenched, all lost for words;
The landing clock, hummocked by shadow, knew it.
Then a blue print frock, loose and talkative,
Spilled, interposed.
The conversation hung by a friendly thread.

She turned. 'Is anything the matter?' 'No.'
Only the fluttering secret a child must keep
Safe for the cold white acreage of sheets,
The moon's barred face:
Cows in the dusk, floating their clouded tongues.

Rain, sibilant on grass, came troubling on.
At night, while the old house cracked its joints
Or shivered its dusty timbers, the fledgeling secret
Broke out its wings.
When morning sun glanced in, his bird was flown.

The Sledge Teams

History is polar,
A texture of webbed silences.

Her violent carnival,
Paraded tongues and costumes,

Bequeath a legacy:
White cerements, a shrouded rigour.

Our eyes ache.
The Blizzard Empires keep their secrets.

Fleshed in crystal,
A few old sledge teams and their leaders

Work each to his crevasse.
Black punctuations of ice,

Snow-blind, undeflected
By our lips freezing as they call.

Summer Palaces

How shall we build our summer palaces?
Will the girls bring us sherbet, and our gardens
Brown to the filigree of Chinese lanterns?

The Emperor speaks in a long robe of thunder,
Bruising us cloudily; his combs of rain
Dance out a dance of more than seven veils.

Islands of bird-music; storm-voices dwindle.
Across the blue, cirrus and alto-cirrus
Draw out an awning for our shade pavilion.

Swallows will sew our flying tents together.
We live as nomads, pitching idle camp
Under the white sheets blowing down the line,

Or swing on ropes to somersaults of grass.
The hasps creak upon our airy gallows,
Roofed by light, floored by a crush of earth.

The strong leaves curtain us; we know each scent,
The deep breaths taken behind swaying curtains.
We have become the citizens of green.

Our walls grow firm in fruit and knots of seed.
A dandelion clock rounds out the hour,
Blowing our time away in feathered segments.

The night lies warm upon a wall of shadows.
We lie as naked in our drifting beds
As the close moon, staining us with silver.

The Cart

It is, after all, only a collection of leaves.
Hours bring them together; ends are not disclosed.
There is the work of hands, felt by their absence.
   They have taught the grasses

But the lesson is lost on them. The birds, though,
Know there is something that they have to do,
It is the way heads nod; they skip the air
   Which is not warm, not cold.

Is this, then, no-place? The wind might say so
As it feels its way through trees, draws down
A gauze of dust at the turning of a path.
   The sky makes itself plain

Upon the ground, and time shapes into seasons.
Their curls are shifted over here and there.
A chrysalis is cooled to the look of life;
   Wings fix, then dry away.

Earth over earth: here is the reliquary
Closed on a wheel chipped from the children's cart.
The talismans are scattered in the courses
   By which light answered them

When secrets were kept and the maze threaded,
The garden spoke with its one feeling voice
Through flowers which denied their own corrosions
   And had no need for names.

CAROL RUMENS

A Marriage

Mondays, he trails burr-like fragments
of the weekend to London
– a bag of soft, yellow apples from his trees
– a sense of being loved and laundered.

He shows me a picture of marriage
as a whole small civilization,
its parks, rosewood and broadloom;
its religion, the love of children

whose anger it survived
long ago, and who now return like lambs,
disarmed, adoring.
His wife sits by the window,

one hand planting tapestry daisies.
She smiles as he offers her the perfect apple.
On its polished, scented skin
falls a Renaissance gilding.

These two have kept their places,
trusting the old rules
of decorous counterpoint.
Now their lives are rich with echoes.

Later, she'll carry a boxful
of apples to school. Her six year olds
will weigh, then eat them, thrilling
to a flavour sharp as tears.

I listen while he tells me about her sewing,
as if I were the square of dull cloth
and his voice the leaping needle
chasing its tail in a dazzle of wonderment.

He places an apple in my hand,
then, for a moment, I must become his child.
To look at him as a woman
would turn me cold with shame.

December Walk
i.m. W. A. Lumley

1

Late winter noon,
the sky blue-black as taxis,
the street below
brimmed with fluorescence.
Typewriters stutter madly
as if they kept trying
somehow to re-shape the words
for bread or anger.
My father stands
in the narrow doorway
where a dim room meets
a darker hall.
His bent hands dangle,
useless even to smoke
a farewell cigarette.
He has only the threadbare
decision he stands up in,
and when they come for him,
no straitjackets or calming
drugs will be required.
Easy as a child,
he'll tiptoe with the strangers
to their white car.
Fled into this city,
this cradling honeycomb
where all the girls shine
and shirt-cuffs are clean,
I know that I have simply
followed him here,
that this could have been his chair.
He stands at my side,
rubbing the cold from his hands,
amused by his child's
new game – the full in-tray,
the memos, the poems –
and saying with his smile:

no hurry, no hurry.
We all have to go home.

2

Pacing behind him,
I imagine how light he must be.
The bearers' tall, black shoulders
would never admit it.
They are braced for immensity.
The organ takes up the pretence,
and the chrysanthemums, quaking
their frilly gold baroque
through icy chapel air.
In plain pews built
too narrow for kneeling,
we remove our gloves
and pray from small books.
He was somebody once,
but sickened, and lost
the weight of himself.
He forgot our names
and wandered for years,
words melting off his back
like snowflakes. Now
as the altar screen slides
tactfully across
to blot out doomed wood,
I recall only a mood,
a flickering of smiled
irony, betraying
that willingness, flat and English
as the whited winter sky,
to be always disappointed.
He was an unbeliever
in everything he did,
yet would have had a hand
in this, perhaps, approving
our boredom, the sad weather
and what there is of ash.

Coming Home

The bar is full of English cigarette smoke
and English voices, getting louder
– a language lumpy as a ploughed field.
It's hard to believe our tongues have got it too.

People are growing drunk at the thought of home.
The sea patiently knits its wide grey sleeve.
No one else comes up to lean on the rail
where, damp and silent, we watch

the long white skirts of land drifting
sadly through mist, as if a young girl sat
by the shore still, waiting for a bluebird.
It's September, and already winter.

And now the toy-sized train
is creeping with its worn-out battery
and a cargo of sandwiches and arguments
over grey-green fields into grey-white suburbs.

We're playing a game with the streets
– spreading them out and tying them up again;
when they've caught us, we're home.
The lawn blows like a tiny English Channel.

We chug towards our own front door
anxiously, seeing as if for the first time
how tight the plot that locks us in,
how small our parts, how unchosen.

The Freedom Won by War for Women

From hassock, cradle-side and streaming walls
– The fogs of faith and wash-day – thin lives beaten
Blank and hung to weep – the fair are gone.
Raw-fingered saints who've tipped their pedestals

And dried their hands at Father Empire's yell,
They chivvy cautious husbands, rebel sons
With bloodiest white. But they'll take the same poison,
Hands deft among his axle-trees and shells.

True warriors, they were furnace-forged when bombs
Jumped roof-high. From tongue to lung the taste
Of lead rolled death. Massed engines pumped their Somme.

It was a flowering and a laying waste
– Man's skills found shining at the heart of woman,
His vengeance, too, expediently unlaced.

A Poem for Chessmen

'Shah maat' – the King is dead

It's like an examination
or some vast dinner party
where the guests sit in pairs
and politely demolish each other.
Your ranks of hunted shoulders
and frowns attest the passion
of the quest. For you are unravelling
a childhood, inching back.
You cross the polite, hushed street
(its pawn cars in rows,
its mitred evergreens)
and softly click the latches
to the room where the grownups stand
as if they'd guessed you would visit
with death in your childish hand.
It's never enough, is it?
However well you win,
however loud your cry
of 'Checkmate, Shah Maat',
King Dad will rise from the dead,
his crown unspilled, his lady
hard-faced at his side.

You mustn't think I'm gloating
nor shiver when you hear
the whispering of my skirts
along the aisles where those
dumb beasts, the backs of your heads,
graze in their sensual doze.
I'm miles from the queening square.
Although no doubt in time
we will change places,
just now you needn't run.
My history is not yours.
Long ago, I set up my pieces
against my father, as you did,
but it was only fun.
Pretty face, I was free to lose.

PENELOPE SHUTTLE

Three Lunulae, Truro Museum

Gold so thin,
only an old woman
would notice its weight

Crescent moons of gold
from the sunken district
of the dark,
out of the archaeologist's earth

The women of the lunulae
threw no barbaric shadows
yet a vivid dance
lit up their bones

I sense the mood
of many women
who wore the new moon
like a necklace

They have got over
the winter
while I still freeze

The slight quick tap
of a clock
goes on
like the rhythm
of an insect's leg
in the grass

I linger
in the locked room
of the gold,
trying to see,
beyond the sickle shapes,
the faces of three women

Sharp shadows breathe hard,
shedding skins like dusty snakes
Light twists in a violent retching

For an instant
there is the fragment of a lip,
an eyebrow fine as a spider's threat

A face like a frost fern

The custodian
locks the lunulae
in the safe once more

Cornish, they are,
he says,
dug up at St Juliot,
regalia of this soil,
and not for the British Museum

You buy me
a postcard of the lunulae
and we leave the museum,
enter the thin gold remains
of autumn

Downpour

A strong rain falls, a bony downpour.
The waters roar, like a riddance.
The day vanishes suddenly
and it is night that hesitates on a brink
for fear of difficulties. The rain, for instance.

Through the letter box, leaves instead of letters,
wet leaves blown along the path
and seeping through the low letter box,
an invasion that comes slowly,
but helped by the rain. The downpour.

I dream of thorns, aeroplanes and red horses,
but seldom of rain.
The creature spinning webs to catch its prey,
I dream of her also
but almost never of rain. The webs of rain.

The rain does not slacken. It has the scent
of mistletoe. But it is a weapon, thrown.
The windows shine black with it.
I sit watching the knotted bunches of rain.
I do not want to cease watching. Such brawny rain.

But the dry house, its music and its meals,
recalls me from the window,
draws me back from a downpour that is drowning me.
I prepare to turn from the window,
yet remain a moment longer,
looking at the blur of the candle-flame
against the dark glass.

There is the downpour. Here is the uprush of light.

Travelling

Across blue fields to find Satan
White stars above me, roots of fire
I want to unlock the keys of the piano

On volcanic islands I hear the passage
of clumsy adults without wings
I am one of them

Rain falls, many delicate colours
appear in the distance
Satan throws winter across his shoulder

I climb the hodden-gray hills
From the harbour I hear the hoarse
tender warning of the foghorn

There are no dinosaurs drinking
at the river's edge
I stoop, I throw a handful of red earth
into the river
There is no time to write a treatise
on this subject

I looked for Satan in the polar lands
My breath stood solid in the air

Cold seized me by the throat, made me helpless
But I did not find Satan,
could not touch his fiery rank flesh

I laboured in a summer garden
Women and children dressed in garish red garments
watched me

In their hands, they held bunches
of flowers, feathers and branches
Four women came towards me,
they related reminiscences to me until dusk,
and the children sat on the lawn, watching

I stand at the door of the granary
I snuff up the odours of harvest
Behind me, Satan is looking for his women
His jaw opens, extends into a beak
I walk to the edge of a steep place
I am looking down into the second sign of the zodiac
Darkness grows up in black clusters around me

But I step back from that edge
I enter a different darkness, it is the dark of the barn,
the sweet stench of the grain

Fosse

> '... and from the menstrual ditch
> The future runs...'
> (PETER PORTER, 'Three Bagatelles')

I am always on the brink.
As one beginning is dwarfed
and changes colour, reddens,
dies, in fact,
and makes for the dark easement
of earth
that is its and my past,
a blindness of words and counties,
I am at the precipice,
listening secretly to that whisper,
the promise of rank,

the possibility of passwords.
Always on the edge,
always at the frontier,
waiting until my papers are in order,
until I can emigrate.
But I am not authorized yet.
Today I learnt that my key
did not unlock the clasp,
that the combination was not perfect
enough to open the deeply-implanted safe.
So I go on waiting here,
in this embrasure of autumn,
prepared for emergencies.
I am here to correct my mistakes.
These corrections are made in blood,
on the borderland of riddles,
at the brink of encyclopedias
I cannot open and read yet.
I accept the repetition
that is always different,
I accept the enclave of the month.
In my deep roots,
the engrossment of my blood aches,
it is cancelling out
the enchantment I planned
and offering a famine.
Yet it offers other habits.
Its perceptions are a new clarity,
the red geraniums, the yellow sunflowers
throb with beauty and versatility.
This blood is a real thing in itself.
It has its heirs and settlements.
In its environment I cannot proclaim
my hostility for long.
No sooner has the month's answer come,
been feared, hated and then accepted,
danced with, adored,
than the fallow hesitations of myself
are audible again,
I hear the new question and its invitation.
Bleeding this fathomless blood,

I move to the brink again,
joyful, beginning again, celebrating:
the new sputters in me
like a fire trying to catch,
it flickers and burns unsteadily,
jerks like a volley of red arrows.

I wait, on the brink of the blaze.

First Foetal Movements of My Daughter

Shadow of a fish
The water-echo
Inner florist dancing
Her fathomless ease
Her gauzy thumbs
Leapfrogger,
her olympics in the womb's stadium

CRAIG RAINE

A Martian Sends a Postcard Home

Caxtons are mechanical birds with many wings
and some are treasured for their markings –

they cause the eyes to melt
or the body to shriek without pain.

I have never seen one fly, but
sometimes they perch on the hand.

Mist is when the sky is tired of flight
and rests its soft machine on ground:

then the world is dim and bookish
like engravings under tissue paper.

Rain is when the earth is television.
It has the property of making colours darker.

Model T is a room with the lock inside –
a key is turned to free the world

for movement, so quick there is a film
to watch for anything missed.

But time is tied to the wrist
or kept in a box, ticking with impatience.

In homes, a haunted apparatus sleeps,
that snores when you pick it up.

If the ghost cries, they carry it
to their lips and soothe it to sleep

with sounds. And yet, they wake it up
deliberately, by tickling with a finger.

Only the young are allowed to suffer
openly. Adults go to a punishment room

with water but nothing to eat.
They lock the door and suffer the noises

alone. No one is exempt
and everyone's pain has a different smell.

At night, when all the colours die,
they hide in pairs

and read about themselves —
in colour, with their eyelids shut.

An Inquiry into Two Inches of Ivory

We live in the great indoors:
the vacuum cleaner grazes
over the carpet, lowing,
its udder a swollen wobble . . .

At night, the switches stare
from every wall like flat-faced
barn-owls, and light ripens
the electric pear.

Esse is percipi — Berkeley knew
the gentle irony of objects, how
they told amusing lies and drew laughter,
if only we believed our eyes.

Daily things. Objects
in the museum of ordinary art.
Two armless Lilliputian queens
preside, watching a giant bathe.
He catches the slippery cubist fish
with perfumed eggs. Another
is a yogi on the scrubbing brush.
Water painlessly breaks his bent
Picasso legs.

Clothes queue up in the wardrobe,
an echo to the eye, or a jangle of Euclid.
The wall-phone wears a pince-nez
even in the dark – the flex
is Jewish orthodox.

Day begins.
The milkman delivers
penguins with their chinking atonal fuss.
Cups commemorate the War
of Jenkins' Ear.
Without thinking, the giant
puts a kettle on the octopus.

The Butcher

*'And even St George – if Gibbon is correct –
wore a top hat once; he was an army contractor
and supplied indifferent bacon'*
(E. M. FORSTER, *Abinger Harvest*)

Surrounded by sausages, the butcher stands
smoking a pencil like Isambard Kingdom Brunel . . .

He duels with himself and woos his women customers,
offering thin coiled coral necklaces of mince,

heart lamé-ed from the fridge, a leg of pork
like a nasty bouquet, pound notes printed with blood.

He knows all about nudity – the slap and trickle
of blood, chickens stripped to their aertex vests.

He rips the gauze from dead balletic pigs,
and makes the bacon slicer swish its legs.

How the customers laugh! His striped apron
gets as dirty as the mattress in a brothel . . .

At 10, he drinks his tea with the spoon held back,
and the *Great Eastern* goes straight to the bottom.

The Grocer

'the Kingdom of God cometh not with observation'
  (James Joyce to Lady Gregory)

The grocer's hair is parted like a feather
by two swift brushes and a dab of brilliantine.

His cheesewire is a sun-dial selling by the hour.
He brings it down at four and five o'clock,

the wooden T gripped like a corkscrew.
Greaseproof squares curl in diamonds on a hook.

He takes, and orientates the chock of cheese,
swoops his hand away, leaves it on the choppy scales.

Tortoise-necked, he reads the price aloud
and fingers do their automatic origami.

He shakes the air into a paper bag and,
eggs pickpocketed inside, trapezes it.

Coins are raked with trident hand,
trickled into the till – palm out,

with thumb crooked over the stigma,
he smiles like a modest quattrocento Christ.

The Behaviour of Dogs

Their feet are four-leafed clovers
that leave a jigsaw in the dust.

They grin like Yale keys and tease
us with joke-shop Niagara tongues.

A whippet jack-knifes across the grass
to where the afghan's palomino fringe

is part Opera House curtain, part
Wild Bill Hicock. Its head

precedes the rest, balanced like
a tray, aloft and to the left.

The labrador cranks a village pump,
the boxer shimmies her rump,

docked to a door knocker, and
the alsatian rattles a sabre –

only the ones with crewcuts fight.
Sportif, they scratch their itches

like one-legged cyclists sprinting
for home, pee like hurdlers,

shit like weightlifters, and relax
by giving each other piggy backs . . .

A Cemetery in Co. Durham

The stones line up in corrugated rows
like a game of *Dover Patrol*
and the ground is full of pencil boxes.

But YOUNG CHILDREN ARE NOT ALLOWED
WITHOUT SUPERVISION because
this is where the adults play.
They to and fro to a chirping tap
and fill the rusty watering can.
The urns are pretend poppy pods . . .

Untidy as a nursery floor, with toys
and little furniture, it is a good place
to come and talk like a child to yourself –
no one is listening.

Ivy clambers over the sides of a rusty cot.
There are snails and scabs of lichen –
things to pick at while you read.
& CHILDREN-IN-ARMS ARE NOT ADMITTED
TO FUNERALS

unless a father pays the bill
for a satin box of buried treasure –
the feel of a fontanelle, buttocks
tender as a soft-boiled egg, and all
the inventory of little flesh.

Each gothic window is like an ironing board.
Mothers touch the pointed stones
as if they were irons.
They never lose their heat –
always burny, always burny . . .

Flying to Belfast, 1977

It was possible to laugh
as the engines whistled to the boil,

and wonder what the clouds looked like –
shovelled snow, Apple Charlotte,

Tufty Tails . . . I enjoyed
the Irish Sea, the ships were faults

in a dark expanse of linen.
And then Belfast below, a radio

with its back ripped off,
among the agricultural abstract

of the fields. Intricate,
neat and orderly. The windows

gleamed like drops of solder –
everything was wired up.

I thought of wedding presents,
white tea things

grouped on a dresser,
as we entered the cloud

and were nowhere –
a bride in a veil, laughing

at the sense of event, only
half afraid of an empty house

with its curtains boiling
from the bedroom window.

In the Mortuary

Like soft cheeses they bulge
sideways on the marble slabs,

helpless, waiting to be washed.
Cotton wool clings in wisps

to the orderly's tongs,
its creaking purpose done . . .

He calls the woman 'Missus',
an abacus of perspiration

on his brow, despite the cold.
And she is the usual woman –

two terra cotta nipples
like patches from a cycle kit,

puzzled knees, finely
crumpled skin around the eyes,

and her stomach like a watermark
held up to the light.

Distinguishing marks: none.
Colour of eyes: closed.

Somewhere, inside an envelope
inside a drawer, her spectacles . . .

Somewhere else, not here, someone
knows her hair is parted wrongly

and cares about these cobwebs
in the corners of her body.

Laying a Lawn
for Ian McEwan

I carry these crumbling tomes
two at a time from the stack

and lay them open on the ground.
Bound with earth to last,

they're like the wordless books
my daughter lugs about unread

or tramples underfoot. I stamp
the simple text of grass

with woodwormed brogues
while my daughter looks on,

holding her hard, muscular doll
by its only leg . . .

She hands me a caterpillar
rucked like a curtain, just as

one day she'll bring me teeth –
segments of sweet-corn

in the palm of her hand.
While she faces me, I needn't see

the thin charcoal crucifix
her legs and buttocks make,

only the hair on her body
like tiny scratches in gold,

her little cunt's neat button-hole,
and the navel's wrinkled pip . . .

For the moment, our bodies
are immortal in their ignorance –

neither one of us can read
this Domesday Book.

The Old Botanical Gardens
for Chris and Lucinda

This delicate sapling
still wears a caliper,
and will never get well
or lose its impetigo now,

for the healers have gone
whose hands could cure

the tap with bronchitis
and make the weather fine.

Eglon, the King of Moab,
is dead in his hothouse,
a leaking bag of peat,
his fez on the floor:

the city of palm trees
he possessed has gone,
his summer parlour cold
as a broken iceberg . . .

The botanical gardens
are empty of everything
but grievances, like
an atheist's heaven.

Grave on bare grave,
and a host of placards,
demanding the return
of flowers from exile:

strangers with Latin names
that are shy on the tongue.
They force us to falter,
like a lump in the throat,

though the gardens are gone
and all our futile grief
a scourge of dead ivy
on a cold stone wall.

In the Kalahari Desert

The sun rose like a tarnished
looking-glass to catch the sun

and flash His hot message
at the missionaries below –

Isabella and the Rev. Roger Price,
and the Helmores with a broken axle

left, two days behind, at Fever Ponds.
The wilderness was full of home:

a glinting beetle on its back
struggled like an orchestra

with Beethoven. The Hallé,
Isabella thought and hummed.

Makololo, their Zulu guide,
puzzled out the Bible, replacing

words he didn't know with Manchester.
Spikenard, alabaster, Leviticus,

were Manchester and Manchester.
His head reminded Mrs Price

of her old pomander stuck with cloves,
forgotten in some pungent tallboy.

The dogs drank under the wagon
with a far away clip-clopping sound,

and Roger spat into the fire,
leaned back and watched his phlegm

like a Welsh rarebit
bubbling on the brands . . .

When Baby died, they sewed her
in a scrap of carpet and prayed,

with milk still darkening
Isabella's grubby button-through.

Makololo was sick next day
and still the Helmores didn't come.

The outspanned oxen moved away
at night in search of water,

were caught and goaded on
to Matabele water-hole –

nothing but a dark stain on the sand.
Makololo drank vinegar and died.

Back they turned for Fever Ponds
and found the Helmores on the way . . .

Until they got within a hundred yards,
the vultures bobbed and trampolined

around the bodies, then swirled
a mile above their heads

like scalded tea leaves.
The Prices buried everything –

all the tattered clothes and flesh,
Mrs Helmore's bright chains of hair,

were wrapped in bits of calico
then given to the sliding sand.

'In the beginning was the Word' –
Roger read from Helmore's Bible

found open at St John.
Isabella moved her lips,

'The Word was Manchester'.
Shhh, shhh, the shovel said. Shhh . . .

A Walk in the Country

'Letè vedrai, ma fuor di questa fossa,
là dove vanno l'anime a lavarsi . . .'
(DANTE, *Inferno*, xiv)

The muddy lane
is its own
travel document,

obliterate
with a variety
of stamps

which allow us
this journey beyond
the sewage farm

like a tape-recorder,
whose black spools
turn night and day

as excrement
patiently eavesdrops
on peace.

It is a machine
that remembers
the sounds of nothing . . .

They are burning
the stubble
in the fields ahead,

which is why
the graveyard seems
ringed with fire

and somehow forbidden.
Is it fear
halting my child

so that her thumb,
withdrawn for a second,
smokes in the air?

Or fascination
like her father's?
I bend and watch

the stalks melt
when I purse my lips
for a morbid kiss

and blow a bright,
whispering ulcer
in the blackened straw. .

One swallow
sways on a wire
like a grain

of whiskered barley,
saved from the flames.
Do not be afraid:

there are men
on the roof of the church,
playing patience,

tile after tile,
and here is a man
gardening a grave

methodically,
lost in the rituals
of growth.

His jacket is folded,
lining-side out,
and laid on a headstone

as he tends
to his fainted plants,
carefully unwrapping

the dark, moist newsprint.
Without thinking,
I roll away a stone

with my foot
and find this toad
with acorn eyes

and a brown body
delicate as a drop
of dusty water

yet still intact
and hardly surprised
by resurrection.

CHRISTOPHER REID

A Whole School of Bourgeois Primitives

Our lawn in stripes, the cat's pyjamas,
rain on a sultry afternoon

and the drenching, mnemonic smell this brings us
surging out of the heart of the garden:

these are the sacraments and luxuries
we could not do without.

Welcome to our peaceable kingdom,
where baby lies down with the tiger-rug

and bumblebees roll over like puppies
inside foxglove-bells . . .

Here is a sofa, hung by chains
from a gaudy awning.

Two puddles take the sun
in ribbon-patterned canvas chairs.

Our television buzzes like a fancy tie,
before the picture appears –

and jockeys in art-deco caps and blouses
caress their anxious horses,

looking as smart as the jacks on playing-cards
and as clever as circus monkeys.

Douanier Rousseau had no need to travel
to paint the jungles of his paradise.

One of his tigers, frightened by a thunder-storm,
waves a tail like a loose dressing-gown cord:

it does not seem to match the coat at all,
but is ringed and might prove dangerous.

Baldanders

Pity the poor weightlifter
alone on his catasta,

who carries his pregnant belly
in the hammock of his leotard

like a melon wedged in a shopping-bag . . .
A volatile prima donna,

he flaps his fingernails dry,
then – squat as an armchair –

gropes about the floor
for inspiration, and finds it there.

His Japanese muscularity
resolves to domestic parody.

Glazed, like a mantelpiece frog,
he strains to become

the World Champion (somebody, answer it!)
Human Telephone.

Big Ideas with Loose Connections

These monumental Hs must have dropped here
from some heavenly alphabet.

Upright at opposite ends of a turbulent field,
they point woodenly in the direction of hope.

Giants, the epigones of Uranus,
stamp around in the cold, steaming like cattle.

Their lives are ruled by improbable fictions:
lines, flags and whistles;

a thirty-two-legged spider that wheels and buckles
over the agony of its stubborn leather egg.

From a gusty somewhere, God looks down on a world
perfectly simple. We are in love.

The giants are having fun.
Nearby, a blind man tickles the pathway,

whose white stick marks a cardiogram,
no one but he can follow.

A wriggling, long-tailed kite leaps like a sperm
at the sun, its blurry ovum.

A Holiday from Strict Reality

Here we are at the bay
of intoxicating discoveries,
where mathematicians
in bathing-trunks and bikinis
sit behind the wheels
of frisky little speedboats
and try out new angles
to the given water.

Everything that we see
in this gilded paradise
is ours to make use of:
palm-trees on the marine drive,
nature's swizzlesticks,
stir the afternoon air
to a sky-blue cocktail
of ozone and dead fish.

All day long
the punctilious white yachts
place their set-squares
against our horizon,
as we lie around on mats
and soak up the heat,
cultivating a sun-peel
that grows like lichen.

A restless volleyball
skips between four figures
like a decimal point,
but the ornamental beach-bum,

who lives under an old boat,
picks at his guitar
and contemplates the plangent
hollow of its navel.

In the hotel bar,
alcoholic maracas
and, on a high glass balcony,
a pompous royal family
of apéritif bottles . . .
Ernesto the barman
tots up a long bill,
castanetting with his tongue.

Utopian Farming

*'Every nation is to be considered advisedly,
and not to provoke them by any disdain,
laughing, contempt or suchlike, but to
use them with prudent circumspection, with
all gentleness, and courtesy.'*
            (SEBASTIAN CABOT, *Ordinances . . .*)

Great maps of dung obliterate the path –
Elizabethan guesswork, or
the aftermath of Ayrshire cows,
come to give milk in the morning.

Real life resumes, as we follows them,
browsing with brooms,
to smudge away these new-found continents,
suds of urinous seas.

Our delicate tubs of fecundity
never quite know which way to go,
hung between legs with swashbuckling,
cream-bag udders, in lieu of rudders.

With kohl-eyed figureheads, beautiful
and dim – if they prance
out of line (manoeuvring sideways),
we morris-dance them back as we can.

Meanwhile, the pigs comport
themselves in their sties like Falstaffian
generals, slumped
with buckled muzzles and small, pouched eyes.

We are like sutlers, bringing them water and nuts,
or leaning down to tickle their flanks,
white bristles stiff, as if
from years of soldierly grooming.

Our service seems a kind of a meditation,
and meditation akin to ridicule.
I love to be here, private,
subversive and free, in friendly company,

where pigs on tip-toes
piss with such a haunted look,
you'd swear there was something amiss,
and sleep-walking cattle dump wherever they go.

Hens are galleon-hulled: we take them by storm,
plucking the eggs from under their bodies,
bony and warm – freebooters against
a proud and panicky-wheeling armada.

From an Idea by Toulouse-Lautrec

Broad beans out of their bath
come to us wrinkled like finger-ends.

They wait on a plate for our solemn
attentions, the ointment of butter.

A syncretic eucharist, supper:
here are two haloes from Denby,

and here, the apparatus
of augury, knives and forks.

Gently, St Laurence does
to a turn in the oven, exuding

incense, garlic and cloves,
the gourmet's odour of sanctity.

Come, let us eat and talk
and be silent together. Our table

is graced by a single chorister –
salt in a fluted surplice.

A Valve against Fornication

Biblical families begat, begat . . .
Aunt So-and-so, sprigged out in a prodigal hat,
swoops on the birdie with her eagle eye –
poor, blurred Aunt Sally, one
(and but one) of a claque of maudlin
country-churchyard hens.

Now time has trumped another resurrection
out of this ample ground, where guests
of a wedding wander the graveyard.
We are like broad
sunflowers of empty circumspection,
touched and turned by the everlasting sun.

Deucalion flung this rubble
down on the grass: family headstones,
rolls of the gentry dead.
We pat them on the back, as if they were dogs;
or crouch to read such recondite catalogues:
names in a babel of chiselling, cryptic
runes of the weather, blotting-paper script.

Here is our vicar in his laundered smock,
trying to shake the hands of all his
rambling flock, while Bo-peep
bridesmaids totter round his feet.
We are the famous human Venn diagram, where
two family circles coincide
in bridegroom and bride.
Bells go mad, living so near to heaven.
Speaking with tongues, they summon and send us away.

Canapés and circuses, of course!
                                    But why

have all these gentlemen come,
wearing the same disguise, with every
waistcoat-W unbuttoned so,
every top-hat fished from a velvet drum?
Waiters juggle by with trays.
Give me a plate of cataleptic
shrimps on thumbs of buttered bread.

Pea Soup

A hecatomb;
haruspication of pods . . .
It is thus that we understand
our kitchen gods –

workaday hierophants,
opening each green victim
with a neat jab of the thumb,
cascading entrails

(like so many plump suspension-dots)
into a deep pan.
Our recipe book
is the Book of Fate,

to be interpreted wisely
and with some imagination.
The shiny china look
of a raw hambone,

the floe of fat
you scrape with a tablespoon
from quivering stock,
one moment's ghost of salt

and a wincing lemon
must all be rightly noted.
The gods are not mocked!
We are expected

to follow their fickle games,
before launching
our rich domestic cargo
upon those blue, blustering flames.

A Disaffected Old Man

The spider in her hanging theatre;
the patient villainy of cats:
the afternoon foretells disaster,
now we have time to sit and watch.

Outdoors, lulled by the sun, I berce
the sticky brandy in my glass
and contemplate the apple-tree,
that writhes like a family history.

My grandchildren are playing cricket
with a beachball and tennis-racket.
My ancient wife sits on my left.
Leaning, we kiss with cigarettes

to make a tremulous bridge for love.
This yawning book. Its foxy breath.
I pluck out phrases like stubborn teeth,
only to mislay them – and soon enough.

Now yoked to her bib, a baby crawls
a number of yards, but then stalls,
seeing the next-door cat dash past
with his foolish, fat, feathery, false moustache.

Bathos

Yes, I had come to the right place: the jumbo
cheeseplant languishing at a window told me,
and the lift's bisecting doors confirmed it.

Emboxment and apotheosis followed
at once. I approved the fragrance of a late
cigar, while numbers counted themselves discreetly.

Time to remember the whole of my wasted life:
evenings of apathy; vague, extravagant walks;
the cat bemused by my keyboard melancholias.

And now this feeling, as if I had been deftly
gathered into an upward oubliette,
to arrive – where? – at a meadow of sulphurous carpet.

There was a young girl at her desk with three
telephones. I spoke to her politely. Magic!
I heard: 'Mr Dixon will be with you shortly.'

A huge vase full of plastic flowers stood
on a ledge, where an old man, passing, bent to savour them.
The unregenerate minutes turned and turned.

Of Mr Dixon's office, I can recall
the photograph of his wife, some freckled apples
and an alarming stuffed owl under its bell-jar.

But everything else has vanished. Stepping out
of the lift, beyond the ailing cheeseplant, I
looked back and wondered if something important were missing.

A Parable of Geometric Progression

The white pretext
for a solemn Tudor dance;

lax, then tautening;

a hammock or cat's cradle
in some playground game-by-rote

of mirror-meeting,

concession and goodbye;
a grave suspense between us;

folding, folding;

this washed and ironed double-sheet
diminishes by halves.

Time brings us, darling,

to such pristine slabs
and a turf-stack of fresh towels . . .

A week-end's washing

crowds about our furniture,
an orderly débris,

as I sit here, knotting

socks into boxers' fists.
How patiently you tangle

with wry triangles, clothing

the family of nobodies
who loiter in our dark.

DAVID SWEETMAN

The Art of Pottery   1945

Teabowl and vase, tray and ewer
stacked in the studio like shapes
fragmented from a landscape: sky
cloudy over the three-colour glazes,
a beach on the crackled oatmeal,
slow seas passing through and across
the rough biscuit – all moods of the tide.

For forty years, Kenji has drawn
melting hands from the grey slip,
begun creation with the actions of death
seeming to strangle the reluctant clay
until it yields, suddenly
as if responding to his impatient foot
stamping, stamping, the clacking treadle.

Today is the never-tired-of moment,
the bank-vault kiln reopened.
And yet, this once, heat and shine
are nothing when behind him breaks a light
brighter than the city's million filaments,
uncountable neon-signs squandering rainbows,
that stripes Kenji the cold white

and midnight blue of a mackerel's belly.
And as this light leaves him,
sagging like a tired dish,
his shadow settles on the nearest bowl
with the merest stroke, almost a letter,
the beginnings of a haiku perhaps
or the fringe of a wave by Hiroshige . . .

Looking into the Deep End

A boy from a village
a nation away from deep water, to him
this was a fascinating parcel, crumpled paper
surface, reflections of ravelled string

though strangely empty. Called
by god knows what palaeozoic urge
he'd stripped and lowered himself in
then tried to walk a length.

But here was no gentle slope, this drop
sharp to the diver's end.
I ran up as they pulled him out, stopping
not at the baby-drool from mouth and nose

more at the darkness, a shadow
between his legs suggesting the outline of Africa,
that brought back those guilty explorations
of childhood that boys share, raising too

a day when I watched my father turn a stone
as if slowly opening a child's sarcophagus, empty
except for the blue-grey woodlice
lying like ampoules pallid with imagined sins –

all hastily reinterred again,
for when they had tidied away
the drowned boy, I dived cleanly
into the deep end and the world,

to my lensless eyes, returned
to that innocent game of green-tiled chess
that sun and water play
with boneless, shifting pieces.

Cold Beds

Thirty years she had waited for disaster
and when they told her he had drowned
she nodded. Like things seen in Holy prints

there had been signs: the greengrocer
piling bound asparagus as if to burn a saint
made her cross herself quickly.

And when she took flowers for Bob
a dead gull lay on the boy's grave,
plump and grey as the shell that killed him.

So now the father's gone, after thirty years
on a bed too big for one she sees it all:
the sails becalmed at the window,

her Madonna for a prow, the moonlight
that gives their walnut cupboard the pattern
of waves closing over his head.

0900hrs 23/10/4004 BC

Lizard-pouchy, wading off Dartmoor
his rifle balanced to assay its worth
and when he pushes his beret up
blackened features end like a lopped egg.

A fisted cigarette gutters, first fire
in a shallow cave, first defence
for the streets of bright houses
each a face, unaware of fear, being ninety

or nothing in an instant. Light now,
where Friesians wait milk-heavy,
their continents a reminder of half a world
waking, a suicide club. The sun picks out

the anorexic puppets dangling to the horizon,
simpletons who carry the screams of the powerful
in a language of chattering teeth. Grumbling,
a jeep comes, its aerials fishing hope

from the sharp air; yes, this violence
is everywhere possible but today elsewhere,
not here in this treasury of gold-
dusted gorse far from the target cities.

Coasting

There is a climate of failure,
clouds imploded like useless chimney stacks,
while on the beach the sandworms
put out spaghetti for the neighbours
though no one eats.
A lazy length of hawser can't spell
even one of the names of Allah correctly
and there's the sinking feeling that comes
from seeing the lifeboat tracks going on and on
into the water, tramlines to Atlantis.

Like the bored teenagers on the promenade
the sea too keeps trying to run away,
off to London and the bright lights,
but always failing, failing, failing . . .
Always pulling back at the last moment.

MEDBH McGUCKIAN

Slips

The studied poverty of a moon roof,
The earthenware of dairies cooled by apple trees,
The apple tree that makes the whitest wash . . .

But I forget names, remembering them wrongly
Where they touch upon another name,
A town in France like a woman's Christian name.

My childhood is preserved as a nation's history,
My favourite fairy tales the shells
Leased by the hermit crab.

I see my grandmother's death as a piece of ice,
My mother's slimness restored to her,
My own key slotted in your door –

Tricks you might guess from this unfastened button,
A pen mislaid, a word misread,
My hair coming down in the middle of a conversation.

The Hollywood Bed

We narrow into the house, the room, the bed,
Where sleep begins its shunting: you adopt
Your mask, your intellectual cradling of the head,
Neat as notepaper in your creaseless
Envelope of clothes, while I lie crosswise,
Imperial as a favoured only child,
Calmed by sagas of how we lay like spoons
In a drawer, till you blew open
My tightened bud, my fully-buttoned housecoat,
Like some Columbus mastering
The saw-toothed waves, the rows of letter 'm's'.

Now the headboard is disturbed
By your uncomfortable skew, your hands
Like stubborn adverbs visiting your face,
Or your shoulder, in your piquancy of dreams,

The outline that if you were gone,
Would find me in your place.

The Gardener

Most like there was an orchard where my woodlot stands,
Kept by some turn-of-the-century gardener who knew
The ways of birds, how sparrows cannot open sunflower pods,
How ash-trees will bring finches to your gate; who trained
The fruiting arms of ever-bearing raspberries, and covered them
With cottonseed and cheesecloth through the see-sawing
Temperatures of March, till honey-dipped, they strained
As low as Driscoll's muscadines, the wineberries you gather
On Meeting House Road without getting out of your car.

No wren has darkened the door of my wren-hut, though I make
Pin-money from my young tomato plants, return a little sea-struck
From my fall trips through the Pine Barrens, or the Finger Lakes:
I could stage a breakdown, smash my blue jardinière,
My hen-on-nest, my amber-bottled vitamins, or else
Revolve the classics in the bookcase from my nursing chair
Till I'd be born again into that warless world, and think
I loved him, entering the parlour at noon, unattended,
With 'The Voice that Breathed Over Eden' being sung.

The Flitting

'You wouldn't believe all this house has cost me –
In body language terms, it has turned me upside down.'
I've been carried from one structure to the other
On a chair of human arms, and liked the feel
Of being weightless, that fraternity of clothes . . .
Now my own life hits me in the throat, the bumps
And cuts of the walls as telling
As the poreholes in strawberries, tomato seeds:
I cover them for safety with these Dutch girls
Making lace, or leaning their almond faces
On their fingers with a mandolin, a dreamy

Chapelled ease abreast this other turquoise-turbanned,
Glancing over her shoulder with parted mouth.

She seems a garden escape in her unconscious
Solidarity with darkness, clove-scented
As an orchid taking fifteen years to bloom,
And turning clockwise as the honeysuckle –
Who knows what importance
She attaches to the hours?
Her narrative secretes its own values, as mine might
If I painted the half of me that welcomes death
In a faggotted dress, in a peacock chair,
No falser biography than our casual talk
Of losing a virginity, or taking a life, and
No less poignant if dying
Should consist in more than waiting.

I postpone my immortality for my children,
Little rock-roses, cushioned
In long flowering sea-thrift and metrics,
Lacking elemental memories:
I am well-earthed here as the digital clock,
Its numbers flicking into place like overgrown farthings
On a bank where once a train
Ploughed like an emperor living out a myth
Through the cambered flesh of clover and wild carrot.

The Weaver-Girl

I was weaving all year, I was closer than you thought,
Though still a comfortable distance from my sun,
Like the goose that summers in Siberia, and winters on the Ganges.

I was your shadow box, your marriage mirror, an unanchored island
Bumping against the mainland, since your arrow lodged
In my hair, and filled my ears of rice with honey

On your twice-monthly visits to my Palace of Great Cold
You had built for me from the cinnamon tree. I stole
Your dish of peaches at the Lake of Gems, you lived

In the Palace of the Lonely Park. My tree grew a leaf
Every day for fifteen days, then lost a leaf every day.
They fell like moon-leaves, like drops from a muddy rope.

My seven openings do not need the saliva of a fox
In a narrow jar – the fox foresees its death with seemliness,
Absorbs its brewing pain – I could reclaim the mulberry orchard

From the sea like the sea-girl with her golden key,
By a magpie bridge, the seventh day of the seventh month,
Unless the swords are stirring in their sheaths:

These days the destructive north is seldom worshipped –
In autumn the tiger descends from the west, smoke
From the burning leaves protects my jewel, yet unnamed.

Next Day Hill

Who knows, you might receive in time for Christmas
A book with primrose edges and a mirror
In the cover. Like a room decorated
At different periods, you will feel it
Like a draught, a shaft of white coming
Long-postponed out of a blue room,
The thin, straight stalk of a woman. It is when
One tries to recount a dream, going on,
Going on, the shyness of other people
Stops mattering, you put it in a cage

Until your lips are quite rested. Is this
Treating a friendship like glass, this great
Temptation to unfold the labour
One had to go through to get back
To the proper size? I wanted so much
To get down again to a place full of old
Summers, Mexican hats, soft fruitwood
Furniture, and less moon, the porch-light
And the leaves catching one another's glance,
Firm clouds not pulled out of shape by wind.

But I am writing here in the dark
Purple sitting room, the buttons scarcely meeting
On my pink shirt with the pearl collar,
The baby near the stove feeding
Strawberries to our ancient tortoise,
As if neither could go to the other:
Upstairs, the hard beds, the dimity
Curtains, the dreadful viking strain
Of the study's brick floor where
My poems thicken in the desk.

I am waiting like a sundowner
For the gift of all travel, the first
Steering star, or a man turned down
Forever by the only girl – call her
Elizabeth, he soaks himself in the comfort
Of her name till a kind of mist
Covers the sky that's all exposed,
A gallant white, inside and out,
And gathers its spine to wedge itself
Somewhere tight, beyond the reach of the mirror.

Notes on Contributors

FLEUR ADCOCK
Born 1934 in Papakura, New Zealand. Educated at Victoria University of Wellington. Emigrated to England in 1963. Has worked as a librarian and is now a freelance writer. Publications include *The Eye of the Hurricane* (1964), *Tigers* (1967), *High Tide in the Garden* (1971), *The Scenic Route* (1974) and *The Inner Harbour* (1979).

DOUGLAS DUNN
Born 1942 in Renfrewshire. Educated at the University of Hull. Has worked as a librarian in America and England. Lives in Hull and works as a freelance writer. Publications include *Terry Street* (1969), *The Happier Life* (1972), *Love or Nothing* (1974), *Barbarians* (1979) and *St Kilda's Parliament* (1981).

JAMES FENTON
Born 1949 in Lincoln. Educated at Oxford. Has worked as a journalist in England, Vietnam and Germany. Lives in Oxford and works as theatre critic for the *Sunday Times*. Publications include *Terminal Moraine* (1972), *A Vacant Possession* (1978), *A German Requiem* (1980) and *The Memory of War* (1982).

TONY HARRISON
Born 1937 in Leeds. Educated at the University of Leeds. Has done translations for the National Theatre in London, and some of his work has been commissioned by the Metropolitan Company of New York. Publications include *The Loiners* (1970), *The School of Eloquence* (1978) and *Continuous* (1982).

SEAMUS HEANEY
Born 1939 in Co. Derry. Educated at Queen's University, Belfast, where he later lectured. Taught for a year at the University of California at Berkeley, and has also worked as a freelance writer. Now lives in Dublin. Publications include *Death of a Naturalist* (1966), *Door into the Dark* (1969), *Wintering Out* (1972), *North* (1975), *Field Work* (1979) and *Preoccupations: Selected Prose 1968– 1978* (1980).

MICHAEL LONGLEY

Born 1939 in Belfast. Educated at Trinity College, Dublin. Lives in Belfast and works as Assistant Director of the Arts Council of Northern Ireland. Publications include *No Continuing City* (1969), *An Exploded View* (1973), *Man Lying on a Wall* (1976) and *The Echo Gate* (1979).

DEREK MAHON

Born 1941 in Belfast. Educated at Trinity College, Dublin. Has worked as a teacher and freelance writer in Ireland, Canada, America and England. Lives in London. Publications include *Night-Crossing* (1968), *Lives* (1972), *The Snow Party* (1975) and *Poems 1962–1978* (1979).

MEDBH MCGUCKIAN

Born 1950 in Belfast. Educated at Queen's University, Belfast. Works as a teacher at St Patrick's College, Knock. Publications include *Portrait of Joanna* (1980) and *The Flower Master* (1982).

PAUL MULDOON

Born 1951 in Co. Armagh. Educated at Queen's University, Belfast. Works as a producer for the B.B.C. in Belfast. Publications include *New Weather* (1973), *Mules* (1977) and *Why Brownlee Left* (1980).

TOM PAULIN

Born 1949 in Leeds, brought up in Belfast. Educated at the Universities of Hull and Oxford. Lectures in English at the University of Nottingham. Publications include *A State of Justice* (1977), *The Strange Museum* (1980) and a critical study, *Thomas Hardy: The Poetry of Perception* (1975).

CRAIG RAINE

Born 1944 in Co. Durham. Educated at Oxford. Has worked as a lecturer at Oxford and as a freelance writer. Edited *Quarto* 1979–80. Lives in Oxford. Publications include *The Onion, Memory* (1978), *A Martian Sends a Postcard Home* (1979) and *A Free Translation* (1981).

CHRISTOPHER REID

Born 1949 in Hong Kong. Educated at Oxford. Has worked as

Books Editor of *Craft* magazine and is now a freelance writer. Lives in London. Publications include *Arcadia* (1979).

CAROL RUMENS

Born 1946 in London. Read philosophy at London University. Has worked as an advertising copywriter in London, and is now poetry editor of *Quarto*. Publications include *Unplayed Music* (1981).

PETER SCUPHAM

Born 1933 in Liverpool. Educated at Cambridge. Lives in Hertfordshire, where he works as a teacher. Co-founder of the Mandeville Press. Publications include *The Snowing Globe* (1972), *Prehistories* (1975), *The Hinterland* (1977) and *Summer Palaces* (1980).

PENELOPE SHUTTLE

Born 1947 in Middlesex. Has worked as a freelance writer. Lives in Falmouth. Publications include several novels, plays, and a study of menstruation written in collaboration with Peter Redgrove, *The Wise Wound* (1978). Her first full-length collection of poems was *The Orchard Upstairs* (1980).

ANNE STEVENSON

Born 1933 in Cambridge of American parents, brought up in America. Educated at the University of Michigan. Has worked as a teacher and freelance writer in England and America. Lives in Hay-on-Wye. Publications include *Living in America* (1965), *Travelling Behind Glass: Selected Poems* (1974), *Correspondences* (1974) and *Enough of Green* (1977).

DAVID SWEETMAN

Born 1943 in Northumberland. Educated at the Universities of Durham and East Africa. Has worked as a publisher's editor in Paris. Now works for the B.B.C. and lives in London. Publications include several books for children, and a historical biography. His first full-length collection of poems was *Looking Into the Deep End* (1981).

JEFFREY WAINWRIGHT

Born 1944 in Stoke-on-Trent. Educated at the University of

Leeds. Has worked as a teacher in England, Wales and America. Lives in Manchester and works at the Polytechnic. Publications include *Heart's Desire* (1978).

HUGO WILLIAMS
Born 1942 in Windsor. Has worked as a freelance writer. Assistant editor of the *London Magazine* 1966–70. Lives in London. Publications include *Symptoms of Loss* (1965), *Sugar Daddy* (1970), *Some Sweet Day* (1975) and *Love Life* (1979).

Acknowledgements

Thanks are due to the copyright holders of the following poems for permission to reprint them in this volume:

FLEUR ADCOCK: for 'The Ex-Queen among the Astronomers', 'The Soho Hospital for Women' and 'A Walk in the Snow', from *The Inner Harbour* by Fleur Adcock. Copyright © Fleur Adcock, 1979. 'A Surprise in the Peninsula' and 'Against Coupling', from *High Tide in the Garden* by Fleur Adcock. Copyright © Oxford University Press, 1971. All reprinted by permission of Oxford University Press.

DOUGLAS DUNN: for 'Men of Terry Street', 'The Clothes Pit', 'On Roofs of Terry Street', 'A Removal from Terry Street', 'Modern Love', 'In the Small Hotel', 'Little Rich Rhapsody', 'An Artist Waiting in a Country House', 'Gardeners', 'The Come-on', 'Empires', 'Remembering Lunch' and 'St Kilda's Parliament'. Reprinted by permission of Faber & Faber Ltd, from *Terry Street*, *The Happier Life*, *Love or Nothing*, *Barbarians* and *St Kilda's Parliament* by Douglas Dunn.

JAMES FENTON: for 'The Kingfisher's Boxing Gloves', from *Terminal Moraine*. Reprinted by permission of Martin Secker & Warburg Ltd. 'The Kingfisher's Boxing Gloves', 'A Vacant Possession', 'A German Requiem', 'In a Notebook', 'Nest of Vampires' and 'A Staffordshire Murderer', from *The Memory of War: Poems 1968–1981* by James Fenton, to be published by Salamander Press and reprinted with their permission.

TONY HARRISON: for 'The Nuptial Torches', from *The Loiners*. Reprinted by permission of *London Magazine: A Review of the Arts*. For 'On Not Being Milton', 'The Rhubarbarians', 'The Ballad of Babelabour', 'Book Ends' and 'Me Tarzan', from *The School of Eloquence*. 'Turns', 'Timer', 'Long Distance', 'Marked with D.' and 'Self Justification', from *Continuous*. All reprinted by permission of Rex Collings Ltd.

SEAMUS HEANEY: for 'Churning Day', 'At Ardboe Point', 'Broagh', 'Anahorish', 'Mossbawn: Two Poems in Dedication – 1. Sunlight, 2. The Seed Cutters', 'Funeral Rites', 'The Tollund Man', 'Punishment', 'Strange Fruit', 'A Constable Calls', 'Exposure', 'Casualty', 'The Harvest Bow', 'The Otter', 'Glanmore Sonnets' I, V, VIII and X, and 'Leavings'. Reprinted by permission of Faber & Faber Ltd, from *Death of a Naturalist*, *Door into the Dark*, *Wintering Out*, *North* and *Field Work* by Seamus Heaney.

CHRISTOPHER REID: for 'A Whole School of Bourgeois Primitives', 'Baldanders', 'Big Ideas with Loose Connections', 'A Holiday from Strict Reality', 'Utopian Farming', 'From an Idea by Toulouse-Lautrec' and 'A Valve against Fornication', from *Arcadia* by Christopher Reid. Copyright © Christopher Reid, 1979. Reprinted by permission of Oxford University Press. 'Pea Soup', 'A Disaffected Old Man', 'Bathos' and 'A Parable of Geometric Progression' are included by permission of the author.

CAROL RUMENS: for 'A Marriage', 'December Walk', 'Coming Home' and 'The Freedom Won by War for Women', from *Unplayed Music*. 'A Poem for Chessmen', from an anthology to be published by Martin Secker & Warburg Ltd. All reprinted by permission of Martin Secker & Warburg Ltd.

PETER SCUPHAM: for 'Early Summer', from *The Snowing Globe* by Peter Scupham. Copyright © Peter Scupham, 1972. Published in the Peterloo Poets series by E. J. Morten Ltd and reprinted with their permission. For 'The Old Pantry' and 'The Sledge Teams', from *The Hinterland* by Peter Scupham. Copyright © Oxford University Press, 1977. 'The Secret', from *Prehistories* by Peter Scupham. Copyright © Oxford University Press, 1975. 'Summer Palaces' and 'The Cart', from *Summer Palaces* by Peter Scupham. Copyright © Peter Scupham, 1980. All reprinted by permission of Oxford University Press.

PENELOPE SHUTTLE: for 'Three Lunulae, Truro Museum', 'Downpour', 'Travelling', 'Fosse' and 'First Foetal Movements of My Daughter', from *The Orchard Upstairs* by Penelope Shuttle, published by Oxford University Press. Reprinted by permission of David Higham Associates Ltd.

ANNE STEVENSON: for 'The Marriage' and 'Utah', from *Travelling Behind Glass* by Anne Stevenson. Copyright © Anne Stevenson, 1974. 'A Daughter's Difficulties as a Wife' and 'A Love Letter', from *Correspondences* by Anne Stevenson. Copyright © Anne Stevenson, 1974. 'Respectable House', 'With My Sons at Boarhills' and 'North Sea off Carnoustie', from *Enough of Green* by Anne Stevenson. Copyright © Anne Stevenson, 1977. All reprinted by permission of Oxford University Press.

DAVID SWEETMAN: for 'The Art of Pottery 1945', 'Looking into the Deep End', 'Cold Beds', '0900hrs 23/10/4004 BC' and 'Coasting'. Reprinted by permission of Faber & Faber Ltd, from *Looking into the Deep End* by David Sweetman.

JEFFREY WAINWRIGHT: for '1815' and 'Thomas Müntzer', from *Heart's Desire*. Reprinted by permission of Carcanet New Press Ltd. Both poems originally published in *Stand* magazine, in 1968 and 1975 respectively. 'A Hymn to Liberty' is included by permission of the author.

HUGO WILLIAMS: for 'The Butcher', from *Symptoms of Loss* by Hugo Williams. Copyright © Oxford University Press, 1965. 'The Couple Upstairs' and 'February the 20th Street', from *Sugar Daddy* by Hugo Williams. Copyright © Oxford University Press, 1970. 'Holidays', from *Some Sweet Day* by Hugo Williams. Copyright © Oxford University Press, 1975. All reprinted by permission of Oxford University Press. For 'Confessions of a Drifter', 'Along These Lines' and 'Tides', from *Love Life* by Hugo Williams. Reprinted by permission of G. Whizzard/Andre Deutsch Ltd.

Every effort has been made to trace copyright holders. We would be interested to hear from any copyright holders not here acknowledged.